Now Different:
THE POWER OF ACTIVE CHOICE

Randy Hampton
Beverly Craddock

Note to Reader
Names and identifying details of some of the people portrayed in this book have been changed to protect confidentiality.

Copyright © 2015 by Randy Hampton & Beverly Craddock
All rights reserved.
ISBN-10: 1507725728
ISBN-13: 978-1507725726
LCCN: 2015901534
CreateSpace, Honolulu, Hawaii

CONTENTS

Preface

Chapter 1	This Is About You	1
Chapter 2	The Active Choice	7
Chapter 3	Can I Sell You Some Happiness?	15
Chapter 4	What An Active Choice Isn't	19
Chapter 5	Riding The Waves of Passive Choice	25
Chapter 6	When What We Choose Meets Reality	31
Chapter 7	Choose a Broader View	39
Chapter 8	Is Happiness a Thought or a Feeling?	45
Chapter 9	The Myth Of Emotional Control	51
Chapter 10	Neutral Is Not An Emotional State	59
Chapter 11	How To Become Positive	65
Chapter 12	Things That Make Us Choose	73
Chapter 13	Choosing the Bad	79
Chapter 14	Feeling Alive	85
Chapter 15	Life… In Retrospect	91
Chapter 16	It's Not About You	97
Chapter 17	Putting It All Together	103
Chapter 18	The Active Choice F-Word	113
Chapter 19	What Happens When It Happens	117
	About the Authors	119

PREFACE

You don't have to go that far back into our past to find both of us working hard for other people. We were making very good money but we were also not fully satisfied with our lives.

From the outward appearance, we had everything we could need or want. We had six-figure incomes, comfortable homes, cars, a boat, and family vacations to exotic places. We had high-profile but high-stress careers.

It shouldn't be made to sound like we were unhappy, in fact, if anything, the opposite was true. We were extraordinarily happy. We'd entered a solid, committed, supportive, mutually-giving relationship and we were happier than either of us had ever been in the past. Despite the joy in our personal lives, we wanted to find a way to spend more time together. We wanted to help people. With those goals in mind, important questions arose and out of the questions came our quest. Could we find a career together that would improve on an already good thing? Could we take personal joy and spread it out from a seemingly limited space into the larger space of a complete life?

In our quest, we found that we were not alone. What would start as a simple conversation with a co-worker about job satisfaction would become a de-facto counseling session when they learned that we too longed for something new, something different. The neighbors, co-workers, friends and family members who grew interested in our quest became even more interested as we began to fill in the details of our future. They became inquisitive - not just about the details of what we wanted to do - to be - but, more importantly, they became inquisitive about the "how" of what we were doing.

For us, it seemed easy at times. We probably just never stopped to think about the fact that we were having a yard sale and selling everything we had accumulated over the past four decades so that we could run away to Hawaii with a grand total of five suitcases worth of possessions. Despite our comfort with the concept, others seemed shocked, and then they got curious.

Talking with people about our plan to find a more fulfilling career that would help other people also seemed to draw a connection with those people who were close to us. In the end, we learned more about our friends, colleagues, and neighbors than we'd known in many years of what we thought was close contact with them. They began to talk about their dreams and then they told us why their dreams were unobtainable. The problem was, we were blowing through those barriers they had built in their own mind with such a rapid pace that others began to doubt their own barriers instead of doubting their dreams.

We did manage to pull off our escape. We "found" our happiness. We make less money than we have in a long time but we smile more and hold hands and are remarkably happy. Even with a lower income, we are wealthy beyond our dreams because we recognize - for the first time in our lives - that we have everything we could ever need.

Here's the most important part though: we didn't become happy because of what we did. That's right. We didn't actually "find" our happiness by changing jobs or moving to paradise. We found our happy long before that move occurred. Those things were a byproduct of our choice to be happy. We found our happiness in ourselves. We chose to be happy and watch everything else come together for that end result. We found happiness in the spark in the eyes of other people as they recognized that they could do anything they wanted if they choose to chase their dreams instead of staring at their barriers. We reached something remarkable and rare. We also took copious notes about the stages of our process because our new desired outcome is to help you find your life, your legacy, your destiny, your choice. And that's what this book is about.

CHAPTER 1
THIS IS ABOUT YOU

What would it take for you to be happy? What would it take for you to be satisfied? What do you need in your life to be financially secure? Challenged? Confident? Comfortable? Well? Fulfilled? Make a list.

Now take a look at the list. What would other people have to do to make you happy? What possessions would be the ones that have the power to change your emotional state to fulfillment? What past event would need to be undone for you to be complete? What career should you have pursued in order to actually be challenged?

And how many of those things on your list are there because of an "if only?" "If only I could get that promotion…" "If only we could afford a house in that neighborhood…" "If only I had been raised in a home filled with encouragement…" "If only someone loved me…"

The problem is that most of the stuff on our lists actually has very little to do with our emotional state. None of those wishes, things, or people can actually make us "happy" or "fulfilled." And if they could make us feel differently, the emotional state would only last for a short period of time before the people would let us down, the things would wear out or lose their shine, and the joy would be lost. As people, we've been chasing the wrong things.

While many people are busy chasing impossible things, there are people out there who have found their destiny. There are people in poverty who live with the mightiest joy we've ever seen. There are families who have lost love ones through war and they have stopped focusing on living a life full of things and started living a full life, regardless of things. There are people with everything who shock the world by killing themselves because of their desperate search for something more, while there are people with nothing who swear they have everything they could ever need.

The common thread among people who are happy and who own the life they live is that they all made the active choice to be that way. They selected their outcome and then pulled the rest of their life in around that desired outcome. They chose what they were going to be and then they made everything else - their job, their relationships, their belongings, and their thoughts - fit into that very state of being. For them, happiness and fulfillment don't come from things but rather from just having what they have. Their completeness doesn't come from another person but from deep inside their mind, their heart, their soul. The people who seem to be doing life the "right" way, are the people who choose their outcome and then wrap their lives around it.

CHOOSE - It's a simple word, meaning "to select from a number of possibilities." Some dictionary definitions include, "to want, desire, or be inclined." Recognizing that you have the power to choose your life, your attitude, and your outcome, will, quite frankly, change the course of your destiny.

If you want to be something, you have to choose. If you want to do something, you must choose. If you want to stop doing something, you'll have to make that choice too.

Consider life for a moment - your life. A lot of people out there are basically doing the same thing we are doing. We're traveling around the sun in circles, getting older. Many of us wake up in the morning, maybe grab a quick breakfast, head off to work, come home for dinner, watch some TV and go to sleep. Then we repeat that routine day-after-day. Sure, we all throw in an occasional weekend with yard work or camping or dinner with friends. If we're lucky we take a week or two of vacation to someplace special, relaxing, exotic, sandy, or warm.

To be fair, not everyone does it exactly that way. Some people work nights. Some people work weekends and holidays. Some people can't afford to take a vacation. Some people work all the time and don't take vacations. Some people are unemployed. Some people are homeless. Some people don't watch TV. Some people are so wealthy that they don't have to work at all.

Despite the subtle or wide differences in the way we all pass the days, there's an all too common theme: most people are looking for a better way. Rest assured - it exists. Once you learn the power of choice, you'll start to do all of the little things differently and it will make a huge difference.

Do you want to make more money? Do you want to work fewer hours? Do you want to spend more time with your kids? Do you want to retire early? Do you want to sing better? Do you want to learn a foreign language? Do you want to be happy? Do you want to have a deeper relationship with your partner? Do you want to make a difference in the world? Do you want to have more time to volunteer at your church, the museum or the zoo? Do you want to live in the big city? Do you want to own a farm? Okay. You can do that. First, though, you have to CHOOSE to do it.

Choosing isn't about wishing. Choosing isn't about wanting. Choosing isn't about making a list of the pros and cons. It's about consciously and then subconsciously committing your energy towards the things you have chosen. It is setting out down the path with the belief that you are meant to already be exactly where you have chosen to go.

Making a choice involves deciding your priorities. You've got to choose what you want by picking it above all of the other things that are alternative choices. And, unfortunately, this is where most of us bog down. The minute we decide what we want or who we want to be, we realize that it means that there are other things we might not get to be. The analysis of the alternatives becomes paralysis.

I want to be wealthy but that would mean risking everything with an invention or a business idea, and that would mean risk, and that would mean… whatever. I want to be a writer but that would mean actually finishing a writing project which would mean spending more time writing which would mean spending less time doing… whatever. I want to have more time to spend with my grandchildren but that would mean taking a lower paying job and selling the house to live closer to them but that would mean that I would miss the Tuesday night…whatever at whatever. The analysis of the options puts an end to people's dreams before they even begin to dream them.

Be honest with yourself. You've decided NOT to do more things than you've ever decided to actually do. Somewhere along the path of your life you became afraid to make the really big choices because all of the other possibilities or all of the potential sacrifices overwhelmed your brain. Think about that for a second, though. The possibilities and potentials didn't overwhelm your dream, they overwhelmed your brain. The possibilities - failure, risk, reward, supply and demand, needs, bills, other people's feelings, work, education - all overwhelmed a part of your body over which you are supposed to at least have some small level of control.

If you're reading this book, then you've probably done the "life math" in your own mind. And you've probably come to a certain set of conclusions:

- What if I choose to start a business based on my really good ideas but find out that it doesn't provide the same income as my steady, stressful, health-insurance-providing, 8-to-5 job?
- What if I choose to spend more time with my family and find out that it means that I'll spend less time doing the other stuff that I enjoy, like playing...whatever.
- What if I try to learn Chinese and I miss all the new episodes of whatever TV show everyone is watching? And I'm not sure I like Chinese television shows. And I don't even know if I'm smart enough to learn something new at my age. And... whatever.
- What if my relationship is too far gone to bring it back, even if I try more? What if she's no longer in love with me but she's already in love with... whoever?
- What if I quit my job and move to Hawaii because I think I can write a book? Wouldn't that be foolish? And scary? And risky? And what if I don't actually know how to write? What if nobody buys books about... whatever?
- What if I start a business and fail because nobody buys... whatever?
- What if I stop drinking and nobody likes me anymore because I'm... whatever?

Sometimes the questions that come from the analysis process are enough to make you want to go back to bed for a few months with a bag of potato chips and a bottle of... whatever. Some people have chosen that approach and discovered - unsurprisingly - that it didn't help. If you're reading this book, hopefully you're ready to expect something different. And it all starts with making a choice

- a choice to be happy, healthy, wealthy, in love, in the movies, debt-free, or... whatever.

So, go ahead and make that list of what it would take to make you happy, wealthy, healthy, self-employed, a rockstar, a writer, a pro golfer, more confident, or whatever. Let's see how many of your barriers are real and how many are paper tigers created to keep you "safe."

Next to each item on your list, write down the things that stand in your way. What's keeping you from your desired outcome?

Put your list away. After you read each of the next chapters, take another look at the list and make any changes that seem appropriate for you.

CHAPTER 2
THE ACTIVE CHOICE

When we talk about choosing to live your life in a certain way, many people express confusion about the action of making a choice. After all, aren't we all choosing things constantly? I choose kinds of pizza or brands of vodka or what show to watch on TV. Haven't I chosen where to live, where to work, and, even, who to love?

Those are absolutely choices we all make, some of them on a daily basis. We live in a modern world filled with convenience, technology, and options. But there's a radical difference between those choices and the kind of choices you should be making. There is a difference between making passive selections and actively choosing how you live, who you want to really be, and what you want to have in your life. It's one thing to pick something while it's entirely different to actively choose who you will become in spite of the selections you have made in the past.

Let's put it this way... most people are making choices and then hoping that they made the right choice. We make the selection but then we let the selection dictate the outcome. A better way is to choose the outcome.

Too often we pick the job we want and we hope that it always pays well, feeds our passion, offers us some growth, and makes us happy. We pick a meal from the lunch menu and hope it tastes good, fills us up, and makes us happy. We select a partner and then we put it all in their court - will they make us happy? In all of these examples, you've made a passive selection but you have not made an active choice. If passively selecting things and hoping they will make you happy sounds like your life, this book will show you why you should instead make the active choice to be happy and then bring those other things in line with that decision. It isn't necessarily easy to do, but it is definitely an easier way to live and the results are so much better.

Making an active choice is about choosing to be passionate and challenged as a person, regardless of the job you select. Whether you're taking an entry-level position, a part-time job at a fast food restaurant, or becoming the CEO of a Wall Street brokerage firm, you are the one who decides what the job provides for you. Sure, someone else is going to set your pay and benefits. The position likely has some established sideboards on what authority you have and the reporting structure. Picking the job is fairly easy because you generally know the specifics and should be able to weigh it against your current job or any other options that might exist. But what will you choose to take into the job and what will you actively choose to take from it? You control the passion that you put into the work and you also control the satisfaction that you receive from doing the work. There isn't anyone out there other than you that can decide if your job makes you happy. You're the one who decides happiness, even in a sea of chaos, strife, and power struggles.

Your boss may tell you that you're doing a great job. Your boss may storm around like a tyrant and tell you that the last person in the position walked on water and you're a miserable replacement. The way other people behave is outside of our control. How we choose to take those things in to ourselves is well within our control. You can choose to work with the passion and integrity that represents you as a person. Choose to let every opportunity in your life generate growth for you as a person and an employee. You may not be in the "right" job for you but you can choose to maximize the experience by learning new skills or finding a mentor in a different department. You can choose to make the work environment better by being more positive and mentoring others. You can even choose to quit and find something that better fits your goals and desires. In the end, you can even choose to stay in a bad job. You can make the active choice to suffer. You can choose to be miserable but you need to recognize that you are making an active choice. You have to choose the miserable - it is not something that can be provided to you without you actively choosing to accept it. It is your choice.

Making an active choice can be as simple as picking something new for lunch and being happy not because you like the dish but being happy that you made the choice to try something new. You may have just discovered that Kimchi or raw ahi tuna is not something you particularly "like." You can allow the resonating flavors of fermenting cabbage to ruin your afternoon or you can choose to be glad that you tried something you'd never tried before in your life.

Maybe you have chosen to be healthy and are bringing your selections in line with that new choice. You can choose a salad and choose to enjoy the flavors. When you choose to be healthy and view food as the source of what you get from your body, you're going to make selections differently - more easily. Making the choice of living healthy or reaching your target weight becomes the priority over being made happy by your lunch. You choose to be healthy and your lunch falls in line with that - regardless of what healthy selection you pick.

When someone asks what you had for lunch, you can make the choice to describe the gory details of Kimchi or the field green salad with vinaigrette. You can also choose to tell them that you went on an international journey or made a healthy choice and tried something amazing. It is worth noting that the choices you make in how you describe your selections to others will also have an impact on how they view the situation. Are you adding to the other person's daily complaint total or is the person being inspired by the way you chose to handle something as seemingly simple as your lunch? You can select your lunch but only you can choose to make everything in your life about your real choices.

If you actively choose to be physically healthy, then every meal selection can become about furthering you toward the goal. You can select a diet program but only you can choose to be healthy and fit. There are so many people out there that bounce from fad diet to fad diet, waiting for a celebrity to offer the watermelon weight-loss plan or some doctor to start selling the All Pizza Diet book.

Studies have shown that the diet you select matters less than the attitude you have headed into the weight-loss effort. Choose to be healthy and fit. Make it a life choice. Make it an active choice. Once you've made that destination part of your core being - part of who you are - you're more prepared for every selection that comes along down the path. You're ready to really select a diet and to stick to it. You're ready to pick an exercise plan and stick to it. Once you really make the active choice to be healthy, instead of the passive selection to diet or exercise, you'll be more successful than you could ever imagine.

Think of yourself in terms of the destination, regardless of how you have perceived your body in the past. You have chosen to be a healthy person. You are bringing your daily selections of foods and activities in line with that active choice. Your body is going to follow.

Making an active choice in a relationship isn't about picking a partner, mate or spouse and waiting for your happiness to arrive. You must actively CHOOSE to be happy and then find the right person to share that happiness with you. When you select a mate and hope they bring you happiness, you're very likely to be disappointed. This is one area where time-and-time again, we see people who make a passive selection and not an active choice.

If you find yourself thinking that the next boyfriend, girlfriend, spouse or lover will be the "right" one, you're making passive selections and your happiness could be far away. It is when you choose - actively - to be whole within yourself, regardless of your relationships, that you will find something more meaningful. It is when you value yourself and decide to really live that you will find that you value your current partner in the same ways you did early in the relationship. When you choose to become complete as a single person, you will find that you attract other complete people to be part of your life. Your choice to be happy or to be confident will draw to you the person that is meant to share that with you.

Think of an active choice as one in which you select the outcome - not the things that will lead to the outcome. The things that will lead to the outcome - the deeds that must be accomplished - are things that will generally select themselves to fall in line with your expectations. Choose who you want to be and begin bringing the rest of life in line with that very active choice.

There are a lot of pitfalls in that last paragraph. Every time we give a presentation to a large group about these topics, there's always someone who hears us explain what we mean by active choice and then they stop listening to the rest of what we say. They'll track one of us down after the talk and say things like, "That was great. I've chosen to be rich and now I'm headed home to wait for the phone to ring and the money to pour into my bank account."

You see, we're not saying that the active choice is the end of the process - quite the contrary - it is the beginning of the process. You can't stop reading at this chapter. You can't merely quit with the affirmation. You can certainly make the active choice to be wealthy but the work that follows still must be done. If you're going to be wealthy, and you're starting at "broke," or "just getting by," you've got to have a plan. To become wealthy, you've got to have a career, an innovation, a product, an investment, a rich relative, or one heck of a pile of luck - just don't count on the luck.

Don't become one of those people who spend their food money on lottery tickets, thinking that the mere decision of wealth is enough. Be one of those people who has made the active choice to be successful by believing in their destiny and believing in their product, talent, skill, experience, or pure drive to make that destiny a reality. Choose to be wealthy, if that's what you want, but be ready to put in the time. Be ready to then make your decisions based on that active choice. Once you make the active choice, the nice part is that nothing from that point on will seem like work - even though there's a lot of it to get done. You choose the destination in an active choice but you've still got to start walking to arrive.

When you make an active choice and choose what you're going to be - happy, wealthy, respected, physically fit, whatever - you then have to be willing to put in the effort to get there. Making an active choice is making a commitment to the necessary work. Making the decision to believe in yourself and your ability to achieve above all other options is the start of change - not the end of it.

Choose what you are going to be - who you are going to be - and then begin the process of making it occur. That's making the active choice. When you stop picking the things, the people, the amounts, the ways and the options, and instead choose the desired end result, then you are on the right path. You just need to recognize that you are at the beginning of the path. The difference between now and five minutes ago is that you know where the path leads, what you will accept along the path, and some of the things you'll need to do to get there.

Noah Galloway is a retired Army Sergeant who lives in Alabama. In December 2005, an IED (improvised explosive device) blew off his left leg below the knee and his left arm above the elbow. He was unconscious for five days before waking up on Christmas Eve in a military hospital in Germany. Noah was faced with a choice. He tells Men's Health Magazine (Nov. 2014), "You can choose to be bitter, or you can choose to be better." Today Noah competes in fitness events including Spartan and warrior Dash events, Cross-fit competitions and Tough Mudder races. He exemplifies making an active choice in today's world.

History too holds examples of people who made first a choice and then wrapped the rest of their lives around it. In 1862, Ralph Waldo Emerson wrote a eulogy for famed author and philosopher Henry David Thoreau. Emerson wrote that Thoreau "...chose to be rich by making his wants few, and supplying them himself. In his travels, he used the railroad only to get over so much country as was unimportant to the present purpose, walking hundreds of miles, avoiding taverns, buying lodging in farmers' and fishermen's houses, as cheaper, and more agreeable to him." Thoreau chose to spend his life living by his own rules, taking only occasional odd jobs to supply funds when needed. Some may argue that life was different in 1862, but it is difficult to argue that it was any easier to make the choice to forgo traditional wealth for a man that could have easily earned it through labor or writing. Thoreau chose actively and lived exceedingly.

CHAPTER 3
CAN I SELL YOU SOME HAPPINESS?

If you watch much television, you get a good understanding of what it takes to achieve a goal through passive selection instead of active choice.

Reality show participants believe that winning - or even appearing - will bring them fame, happiness, and wealth. Their entire destiny is based on the whim of a panel of judges, the pretentious gift of a rose, or a vote of "the tribe."

News anchors, reporters, and teams of "analysts" highlight what's wrong with the world each and every day. They serve up horrors and injustices that we must overcome if we are to have any peace in our lives. If we were fortunate enough to conquer all of the ills they bring us today, they'll mix up a new batch for tomorrow's newscast. Watch long enough and you begin to believe that you can't have happiness, love, safety, security, peace, wealth, or anything good because there are so many things that are preventing that from happening.

Sitcoms teach us to laugh at the plight of people who aren't very smart. Characters make mistake after mistake only to find joy after 29 minutes. Sitcoms make the overweight person appear jovial, the young mother appears clueless but well-meaning, and the elderly appear to be loving idiots with hints of sugar-coated generational sexism, racism, or religiosity. While the satire can serve as effective social commentary, it comes in such huge quantities that viewers can become overwhelmed with cynicism for even the simplest parts of life.

Television dramas fix the world in 60 minutes only to start the next week at the same point of brokenness, sinister intrigue, or fearful threat. Many of these shows are based on the dark side of the people who kill, terrorize, or stalk, and the people who hunt them. Watch an evening of crime dramas with a topping of the nightly news and it is quite possible that your faith in humanity, faith in yourself, and faith in a positive outcome can be weakened.

Television isn't bad. There are good things out there to watch. The problem comes when too many of us switch on the television and absently absorb it into our minds. If you're making active choices, it's worth at least asking yourself if the things you are watching are moving you toward your desired outcome or are they just filling space.

If you really want to see what it takes to be "happy," just watch the commercials sandwiched around all that stuff on television. There are thousands of advertisers out there that have what it takes to make you happy. They are all quick to tell you that they have what it takes to make you whole. They have what it takes to make you feel better, smell better, clean better, drive popularly, and become the person you really should be - at least according to the media standard.

And yet you know, deep down, that there isn't a product on this planet that can really make you happy. There isn't a product out there that can make you wealthy - just a bunch that can give you the appearance of wealth. There isn't a product out there that can make you healthy - just a lot that can keep you on the path of trying to be healthier. Passive selections are made through advertising while true active choices are made through your own determination of who you are going to be at the end of the process. Driving the right kind of car is not going to change your outcome. The stuff that you feel on the inside doesn't get fixed by the things in your driveway, your bank, or the mall.

What if you woke up one day and none of that stuff mattered? What if you woke up one day and the only things you wanted were exactly the things you had? What if you were able to look around your room, your house, your office, your life, and know that you didn't really need anything more than what you saw there? Marketers are paid to sell you on the fact that even if you've reached that point in your life where you "have it all," there's still one more thing that you "can't live without."

Regardless of wealth or the inventory of their belongings, most people have been raised to believe that they need something better - something more - to be happy. This theory has been packaged as "The American Dream." If you're chasing that next big house or that next car purchase, then you're living in a world of shortage. You're living in a world where you will never really achieve the end result, because there will always be something else that you want. Maybe your next movie deal will bring the joy of owning a Ferrari but you'll need another movie and another deal to get the yacht and the bigger mansion.

Now, most of us aren't wealthy enough to play in that world of movie deals and Ferrari's, right? Most of us are pretty happy paying the mortgage and maybe affording music lessons for the kids. You read the previous paragraph about needing more and more and you're fairly certain that there's some dollar amount out there where you could walk away and be happy. You're sure that you aren't one of those people that is chasing happiness through wealth.

But are you doing the same thing in your career? Your relationships? Your thoughts? Take a look at your job. Do you find yourself spending a lot of time looking for a "better" job? Are you just sure that the next one will treat you right? Are you sure that your next supervisor will appreciate your talents? Have you found yourself in the never-ending search for happiness through work?

What about the people you date? Or even the person you're married to? Do you secretly know that you could do better? Do you find yourself checking out other potential partners too much? Do you flirt to make yourself feel like you've still got something to offer? It's probably worth recognizing that there isn't another partner out there that can give you what you're looking for if you're always looking for more. Someone can't give you what you can't find yourself. If you aren't happy, there's not a partner on this Earth that can make you happy unless you make the change and actively choose to be happy.

What about in your own thoughts. Do you ever wonder if you're good enough? Attractive enough? Thin enough? Worthy of the things you have - even if you have very few things?

All of these scenarios are really similar. The wealthy person who needs more is just like the job seeker who needs more. The unhappy spouse is in the same boat as the self-doubter, both searching for something more than what they have.

Unhappiness awaits people who have scarcity in their attitude. No matter what you have, what you do, or who you are with… it will never be enough. It can be hard to change the desire to have more. The first step is recognizing our relationship with wanting more, if we're going to make real choices about who we are and who we are going to be down the road.

The ironic thing is that happiness is not scarce. Happiness is quite common. Happiness is abundant. Happiness is a completely renewable resource. Peace, love, joy, wealth, health, opportunity, advancement, and anything you might want to be are also available in large enough quantities that you can have them - you just can't buy them on TV or at the mall.

CHAPTER 4
WHAT AN ACTIVE CHOICE ISN'T

If you're going to make an active choice, it's probably important to understand some things about active choice versus some of the other options.

Active choice is not making a wish. Wishes are great but they probably should be reserved for wells, shooting stars, and birthday candles. You can wish to be a lot of things but wishes alone won't get you there. Nothing truly good is obtained merely by wishing for it. Even those that get lucky enough to pick the right wishing well, generally see their new wish go in the wrong direction quickly because they aren't very invested in the outcome. It was, after all, just a penny and a wish in the well. How many normal-guy-turned-lottery-winner stories have you heard where the winnings were wasted or scammed away only to have the "lucky" winner right back in the poor house - or even worse off - in a very short time. Go ahead and make wishes. It's fun. But you're going to have to actually choose to make things happen.

Choosing isn't just setting a goal. Goals are very important. You'll need to set a bunch of them along the way to whatever you choose to accomplish. But the mere act of setting a goal is not enough. It's not enough because it is merely a statement of a destination. Goals have also become synonymous with falling short. Aiming for the target isn't enough - you've got to know that you're going to hit it.

You may have a goal but you've got to choose to make it a reality. You've got to make achieving the goal the priority. You've got to determine how you're going to get to the goal and what things you're going to set aside in order to achieve the goal. Setting the goal is necessary but it isn't enough to get you there. You can set a goal to complete the Tour de France route on your bike but you'd better choose what you're going to stop doing in order to find more time to train.

Choosing isn't trying, or hoping, or considering. This is "jumping off a cliff into the ocean" kind of stuff. If you're only standing on the ledge to consider the height and the risks, you're going to back down the first time you feel the breeze. That doesn't mean that choosing is about making a foolish choice without considering the implications but it means that once you've considered the implications, there isn't much point in considering them for the 435th time.

History is full of stories of people who decided that they were going to be something and then pulled it all together in spite of some pretty long odds. Tim Westergren provides a recent example. In 1999, Westergren decided to change the way that people were listening to music, so he founded the Music Genome Project. It was an effort to help people find new musicians and bands they might like by creating a system where people could create their own radio stations that played songs that are similar to songs that they already like. With a complex algorithm and hundreds of analysis points in each song, an individual rates the music they listen to and then they hear songs that have similar attributes. The system learns the songs you like as you continue to be able to rate each song you hear.

The technology that Westergren developed has become familiar to more than 200 million Pandora listeners. It has also made Pandora Radio founder

Westergren millions of dollars. But Pandora and its predecessor companies weren't an instant success. In fact, in 2001 Pandora was almost broke. Westergren laid off most of the company's staff. The few employees who stayed on chose to defer their salaries because they believed in the company concept. Four former employees sued after they found out that deferring salary is an illegal practice in California and Westergren was forced to settle their claims by maxing out his 11 credit cards. Most people would have called it quits and filed bankruptcy but Westergren believed in his vision and was passionate about music. It was enough - barely. Investors came along and got Westergren the staff and the funding he needed to see his dream through. Fast forward to 2011 when Pandora went public and was valued at $2.6 billion - that's billion with a "B" - by the New York Stock Exchange.

Another example of deciding that you have something - that you ARE something - even before anyone else acknowledges or sees it can be found in the story of a recently divorced mother who was raising children without an income. She had a story in her mind though. It was a story about a boy wizard named Harry Potter. J.K. Rowling's first Harry Potter book was rejected by twelve publishers and even the one who did finally accept it told her to get a job on the side because "there is no money in children's books."

Rowling can afford a house bigger than Hogwarts these days but she recognizes that jumping in with both feet is required. Speaking at Harvard University in 2008, Rowling focused on failure. That's right, failure. Very few of us would speak of Rowling in terms of failure. "You might never fail on the scale that I did," she said. "But it is impossible to live without failing at something, unless you live so cautiously that you might as well not have lived at all - in which case, you fail by default."

In spite of her success, Rowling recognizes that she had to step into her desired outcome so that everyone else would believe in it. She had to go through what many people see as 'failures' in order to achieve. She had to believe that she was a writer with a story to tell and then bring everyone and everything else in line with that outcome.

Take another look at that list you made of things you want to achieve. Is there a top priority on the list? Can you rank the things you want in order of importance?

Some people will value "wealth" over "time with family." Don't allow other people's or society's judgement to creep into this process. While someone in your family might look at your list and say, "shouldn't family come before money?" This isn't a group exercise. You may know that for you the achievement of a comfortable lifestyle will allow you to provide a college education for your children, a more comfortable retirement with your spouse, and a legacy of good things in your community - all of which you may want.

What is that most important thing for you? Take a few minutes and explore the alternatives to that outcome. Examine what it would take to be the opposite of your choice or to only partially be the thing you want to be.

It can be really beneficial to take a look at all of your options - even the ones you won't choose. If you're making the choice to "spend more time with family," you need to know what other options are available to you in that realm. Write down a few other things you could spend more time doing. What would "spend more time with golf" look like? What would "spend more time on my education" look like? What would "spend more time sleeping" entail? By exploring what the other alternatives would require, you'll get an understanding of the things required for your choice.

For example, you know that spending more time sleeping, might mean going to bed earlier. In that regard, does spending more time with family mean coming home from work earlier? If more time playing golf means clearing your Saturday calendar for a round at the country club, would more time with family involve clearing your

Saturday calendar for family outings?

By examining the other alternatives we can often find clues to help us achieve something that was otherwise difficult.

If you have chosen wealth as your priority, look at what actions would be required for you to be poor and those needed to be middle class. Being poor might involve spending needlessly on "things" and could provide some clues that will help you make decisions about what it takes to be wealthy. If health is your desired outcome, figure out what it would take for you to be obese or unhealthy. Examining the alternative can help better define your desired outcome and assure that it really is the one you want.

Selecting your desired outcome also involves the prioritization of that outcome above the things that prevent you from achieving it. List out all of the things you currently do that are NOT leading to your active choice outcome. There are 24 hours in a day and you're using them up right now. What are you going to stop doing in order to achieve what you want? If time on Facebook or watching sports is keeping you from writing that mystery novel you've been dreaming of completing, then making an active choice to be a writer will mean giving up some of those other things.

If you're going to actively choose to be more peaceful, then you're going to have to eliminate that thing in your life that makes you less peaceful. Make a good solid list of the things that are holding you back.

It is also possible that there are people who are holding you back from achieving the thing you want to achieve. If you are choosing to be happy, you might have to find new ways to deal with the people in your life that are not happy - or are infringing on your ability to be happy. While you can't control that other person, you may need to control the amount of time they are around you or the amount that you let them determine your outcome. Make a list of the people who could hold you back. And add some notes about ways you might have to limit their access to your time or your moods.

What are your own thoughts that are keeping you from achieving your desired outcome? Do you believe that wealth is a selfish choice? Do you think everyone in your family is unhealthy so you are destined to be the same? Do you feel like you're not smart enough or good looking enough to be what you want to be? There's an interesting truth about most of the self-talk that holds us back - it generally isn't true. That's right. You've been lying to yourself. The thoughts that are holding you back are going to need to go too. They can't be part of an active choice.

CHAPTER 5
RIDING THE WAVES OF PASSIVE CHOICE

If you look around your world today, you're likely to see a lot of people passively living their lives. Passive people are easy to find, especially on social media.

Watch among the posts for the people who post every up and down in their life. A happy face is posted because they like their new hair color. A sad face and a vague "some people suck," or "having a bad day," when things aren't serving them well. Many times they post their stumbles because they need someone to boost them up. They live passively and they determine their own value based on the strength or number of responses they get to the fact that they're, ":-(having a bad day."

There is a real problem with passive living. It isn't just that we may ourselves be living passively, the bigger problem is the faith we're putting in everyone and everything else. If we walk around waiting for actions, events or people to make us happy, we are typically going to be exhausted and disappointed. It is much easier to choose to be happy because of and in spite of things, people and events. Doing it the active way leads you to experience a far more meaningful existence.

Other people cannot meet our expectations. In fact, it's unfair to assume that our sister or best friend knows exactly what we need to hear - especially if we only fish for a reply with a sad face emoticon.

We may want someone to say something nice to us. There's nothing wrong with that. From time-to-time, we all enjoy being told that we look good or we're smart or interesting. Many people will seek out a constant supporter - the "go-to" friend - but if that friend is having a tough day, we may not get what we feel we need. It isn't their fault. It's our own fault for having the wrong expectations. Worse yet, if we're living our life with constant need for validation, we're likely to be even more messed up if we don't receive it. We can be a mess to begin with but then we get even deeper in our hole when the people around us fall short of our expectations. In these situations, it is critical that you set your own standard of joy and happiness.

When our friend doesn't comment on our mid-morning "bad day" post, we add a mid-afternoon "let down again," post. When that doesn't elicit the needed 18 likes, two text messages, and a phone call from all the people that care about us, we begin to think that we're even worse off than we thought earlier in the day. Not only did our day start out poorly, nobody cares about us too. By living passively, we've put our happiness in other people's control and we've become even more unhappy when those people don't come through for us.

If you've been riding the roller coaster of emotion, it's tempting to think that you can say, "I'm going to be happy," and let that be the end of it. After all, it would be closer to an active choice if you went that route. Positive affirmation proponents would tell you that just repeating the suggestion of happiness will be enough to help get you there. While positive affirmations are a good way to keep focused on your positive outcome and the daily steps to get there, there is more to it than that. We've got to give up on expecting other people to notice. We've got to be happy, healthy, wealthy, a fireman, or whatever on our own. We can't say, "Be happy," and then wait for everybody to notice our ridiculous smiles because we know how much everyone wants us to be happy.

Happiness is an active choice. We must make the active choice to BE happy - not just to ACT happy. Actors play a role for the benefit of an audience. In the realm of acting, the response of the audience matters. If you choose to act happy, you're merely playing a role, and you're still being passive. You're behaving in a happy manner hoping that your spouse, your co-workers or even you will notice a difference. Maybe they will even change because they will see that we have changed. You act happy and hope that other people treat you better. You act happy and hope that the grocery store clerk is nice and the mechanic goes a bit easier on the bill.

Acting can work. Other people will notice and may react differently - just like they do when an actor plays his part well. The problem is that the actor knows he is acting just like you know that you're merely playing the happy role to serve a purpose. When the purpose is served or a failure is encountered, you're done acting and back to the same place you started the role - unhappy and passive.

What you've got to do is actively choose to be happy - or whatever else is on that list you made. The responses from other people do not matter. While we want to be happy because we know that it makes us better, even to the people around us, we must first be happy for ourselves. Choose to be happy. With no pressure to be anything else or to act happy so that someone notices, your happiness will just begin to grow.

The next time you're thinking about posting something because you need someone to validate your importance, skip the post. Go out and activate your own happy. Close your eyes and let yourself feel happy. You may have to remember a happy time but that happy feeling is right there inside of you. Activating it is a lot easier than waiting for someone else to do it - someone who might need to figure out their own happiness too. Be happy. Then post something for one of your friends telling them how much you appreciate them. You might just help them find their happiness. And then you're not acting, you're actually engaging in happiness.

So what happens when you've decided to be happy and customer #17 has decided that it's his day to be a jerk? You got his order wrong... didn't recognize him instantly... put him on hold... forgot to send an email... whatever. How can you be happy when this guy is reciting a list of all of the attorneys and CEO's that he knows? If you've practiced finding your own happiness, you can even use it in these kinds of situations. Generate your happiness and apologize.

Now that you're working on your own issue, you're going to find that it's easier to understand that other people face challenges too. Customer #17 may not have found his happiness yet. Hang on to yours - regardless of what actions he takes to express his anger. Remember, you can't control what someone else does, you can only control your reaction to what someone else does.

Most people wonder at this point if they can really just choose to be happy. What if lots of bad things are happening in our lives? How can we overcome real emotions like grief, anger, and sadness just by choosing to be happy? Keep reading. We'll explain more in the next few chapters.

Musician Lou Reed is probably most famous for his 1972 album Transformer, which featured the hit song Walk on the Wild Side. In music circles, Lou is most known for his uncompromising approach to music and to life.

Reed's 1975 album Metal Machine Music contained no songs but rather 64 minutes of guitar reverb and avantgarde industrial noise. Some contend the album was completed by a disgruntled Reed to finish out a five-record contract with RCA Records. Others say it was just Reed's way of showing his distaste for what was happening with the music scene at the time. Either way,

Reed did things in a unique way - his way - and he absolutely did not care what others thought.

Reed was a founding member of the punk movement as a member of Velvet Underground and later he was a solo artist who influenced artists like Sid Vicious (Sex Pistols), Chrissie Hynde (Pretenders), Bono (U2), David Bowie, Tom Morello (Rage Against the Machine), and Nikki Sixx (Motley Crue).

When Reed died in 2013, *SPIN* magazine reran a painfully argumentative 2008 interview Reed gave to writer David Marchese. Marchese added a brief updated introduction to the 2013 story:

> "In the wake of Lou Reed's death, do not be fooled into thinking he was a man whose genius was a result of being cool, or of simple recalcitrance. He sang, often from behind impenetrable black sunglasses (which hid indecipherable eyes) about dirty sex and holy drugs when it wasn't yet clear that rock could handle that. He did it anyway. He wrote a song called "I Wanna Be Black." He put out a full-length LP of screeching guitar distortion. ... All of which is to say he did whatever he wanted. The thing was, though, he gave a s*#t. He's gone now, but he gave more than most people could handle or were willing to admit. ... talking to him in person, I realized that the reason he did what he did, and acted the way he acted, was because he cared so much — about music, about his ideas, about communicating."

After Reed's death, his wife, performance artist Laurie Anderson, wrote a letter/obituary to the local paper in East Hampton, New York. She concluded it by saying, "Lou was a prince and a fighter and I know his songs of the pain and beauty in the world will fill many people with the incredible joy he felt for life."

Lou Reed lived his own life, actively. He didn't really spend a lot of his time looking for others to give him admiration. In the end, he left behind a legion of people who thought very highly of him, not because he needed it but because he had lived actively and decided somewhere along the way that he was a musician and a poet, regardless of whether he fit the standard for it that others had developed.

CHAPTER 6
WHEN WHAT WE CHOOSE MEETS REALITY

With the understanding that you need to make active choices instead of passive choices, the next step is to make sure that you're using active choice in the right way. Making an active choice is all about getting all of the things in your life pointing in the direction of your desired outcome, but that doesn't mean that you should ignore everything else in your life.

The theory of choosing your outcome has been expressed by others before, so we don't claim that "deciding to be happy" is some brand new concept. The problem with much of the advice we've read is that some experts advise that you just "be happy" - regardless of what goes on around you. While that's a great concept for accomplishing happiness - or any other outcome - it's not a very practical way to live for most people. Most of us can't just ignore what is happening in daily life. Ignoring challenges has a tendency to make them worse - not better. If you're going to achieve something, you're going to have to do it along with all the other stuff that's going on in your world - every minute of every day.

Advising people to just smile and trudge on happily isn't sufficient. The advice has got to include the ability to deal with "real life." If we ignore our abusive, alcoholic spouse and just keep smiling, it isn't really living actively -

it's living isolated or oblivious. You have to respond to some things - especially those that are limiting your outcome. If you want to be wealthy and your spouse has a shoe purchasing addiction - you aren't going to get there, at least not easily. If you want to be confident but your lover tells you how bad you are in bed, you're going to struggle regardless of how many times you shout your confidence into a mirror each day. Pop psychology's answers of just believing more - or believing harder - too often falls apart when we match it up against life.

If you could go live in a cave every day and not have to deal with other people, you'd have a very good chance of controlling your environment and being able to select your attitude, your emotional output, and your mood. But most of us can't join a monastery or live in a cave. We are out there living and in doing so our world is going to bang into the worlds of lots of other people. Even if we resist that previous urge to seek validation from them, we're still going to encounter people who have needs, values, and moods that may be very different than ours.

It is very important to understand that making active choices doesn't cure everything in your world. Choosing to be happy doesn't mean that you won't encounter difficulty. Choosing to be a writer or a rock star doesn't mean we won't find difficult publishers or agents. Choosing to be more independent doesn't do away with all the people who we were relying on for things in the recent past or the present - and while we may desire our change, they may not honor what we're trying to achieve. Other people are making choices too. They may choose to be mean, inconsiderate, ignorant, difficult, needy, angry, or greedy. Those people's choices will sometimes crash into your reality.

You can't control other people. You also can't control tornadoes, car accidents, cancer, animals, and terrorists. In fact there is a massive list of things that you can't control. Meanwhile the list of things that you can control is pretty short. When the "real" world meets your choices, the only thing you actually can control is how you will respond.

Think about the guy that cuts you off in traffic. Maybe he was running late and about to get fired. Or, maybe, he was just a jerk. Regardless of his reasons or excuses for cutting you off, you can only control your response to his action. You can choose to respond by being angry, frustrated and antagonistic. Or you can make the active choice to recognize that he may have the ability to cut you off but he doesn't have the right to dictate your mood, attitude or response. Those controls belong to you.

Sure, some guy cutting you off in traffic could be a small concern. What if you have real big problems, you ask? What if somebody else hit your car and you wake up in the hospital, unsure if the rest of your family is okay? What about when your mother is diagnosed with Alzheimer's disease? What about when a flood wipes out your family farm? All that advice to just slap a smile on your face and not let those things bother you is a bit hollow in those kinds of times. While there may be some actual benefit from the "just smile" approach, we're not suggesting that you never feel angry or sad.

Anger and sadness are important emotions. It would be foolish to ignore them. Anger should help us recognize that something unfair has happened to us. Sadness reminds us to grieve a loss. Those emotions are not bad. They do not need to be suppressed. In fact, suppressing anger and sadness can leave you with bigger problems sometimes than expressing them.

What we want to suggest is that you express your feelings appropriately. You should express anger in appropriate ways that defend your personal space and stand up for your integrity. You should express sadness through appropriate mourning, which allows for healing.

But what if things just aren't going our way? Can't we just feel sorry for ourselves? Can't we scream at the universe about 'fairness' and fate? Can't we at some point determine that maybe we're just not like other people?

They're the lucky ones. They're the ones who are meant to be happy. What if we're just destined for hardship? What if God has decided that you will face challenge after challenge in your life?

When we hit the point that anger and sadness are no longer serving a purpose but are instead directed inwardly (at ourselves) or broadly (at the Universe, God, fate, whatever), then the emotions are no longer serving us. When emotions cease to function properly, that's the time to engage your smile, your inner strength, your faith, or whatever. NO, you can't just feel sorry for yourself. You may not decide that someone else was meant to be happy and you weren't. No one decides your happiness for you - except you.

You can be angry when someone harms you in some way. You can be sad when something happens to someone you care about. Those are natural reactions. The error comes when we decide - when we make the active choice - that those singular actions or events are somehow allowed to affect other things in our lives. Because we are angry in one area, doesn't mean we should be ruled by anger in all areas of our life.

When a parent dies, we should mourn. We should not, however, decide that our life is over too. Our mourning should not become depression, overwhelming every part of our life, because we can choose to respond in a way that is healthy for us. We can choose to live happily - not because someone died but rather in spite of it. The world is sometimes unfair. The world is sometimes sad. But it is ours to decide if that lack of fairness or that sadness is a blanket that will extinguish our own light. Only we can make that choice. And that means it requires an active choice.

There are moments of sadness, terror, and loss in all of our lives. Choosing to be happy does not ward off the bad things. Choosing to be happy helps you survive them. You can mourn the loss of a friend. That's appropriate. You can also choose to honor their memory by remembering the reasons they were your friend in the first place. You can be sad or even frustrated when the doctor says those test results are cancer. Then you need to choose to fight, to survive, and to do it all with a smile and determination that will make people notice. And if "fight" is not an option, you can choose to live out your last days in a way that will make a difference. You can choose to leave a legacy of bitterness or you can choose to leave a legacy that is something more - something more active, something of your own choosing, not the cancer's.

Maybe your entire life has been angry and frustrating. Your childhood was unfair. Your adult life has been a series of failures, rejections and humiliations. "Life" has dealt you a bad hand. You have chosen to react with anger, bitterness, sadness or depression. Maybe your story is so tragic that no one will ever blame you for what you have become at this point. And no one should. You have likely done the best you could do. But know one thing: the next choice is yours. You can choose to react with a smile. You can choose laughter - even if you don't know how. You can choose to change. Today.

Some people wonder, "Why should I change now?" Or even, "Why should I choose happiness when most people would choose to be angry for this burden?" Those are fair questions. As we've said, no one should blame you for the choices you have made in the past. Unfortunately, every choice you make from this moment forward is your responsibility. Why should you change now? Because you now know that change is within your power. You now know that you can choose something different. That very knowledge means that you have to take responsibility for every single choice you make from here on out.

Why should you choose happiness, contentment, fulfillment, joy, confidence, wonderment, peace, success, strength or health when the other choices are comfortable and familiar? Because coffins are comfortable and familiar. In the history of this planet, no one ever did anything really amazing by being comfortable and familiar.

Real change - real life - requires being uncomfortable and unfamiliar. That means that real life requires making some active choices. It may require working harder. It may require being appropriately unsettled, afraid, angry or sad. But it will certainly require that you actively choose your destiny.

You will not be required to smile your way through saving the world - unless you choose to do that. The decision to make active choices does not come with a huge responsibility to invent or cure or save. It comes only with the understanding that choosing your own outcome is well within your power. You don't have to rescue mankind - though many people have chosen to try - but rather you choose to rescue yourself.

The most compelling work on the subject of finding yourself in the midst of a very harsh reality can be found in Viktor Frankl's 1946 work, *Man's Search for Meaning*. Frankl's book explains how Jewish people were able to survive the horrors of Nazi concentration camps and the hardships that faced the Jewish people when the war ended.

Frankl, himself a survivor of the Auschwitz concentration camp, contends that even in the depths of horrible circumstance, humans can find their meaning - and in doing so find something that even transcends happiness. He stated that mastering "the art of living in a concentration camp" involved the ability of a person to hold onto their sense of humor and to seek love - even the memory of love from those who had died. Frankl would know - his mother, father, brother, and his pregnant wife all died in the camps. "The one thing you can't take away from me is the way I choose to respond to what you do to me," Frankl wrote. "The last of one's freedoms is to choose one's attitude in any given circumstance."

Man's Search for Meaning, a must-read for seekers of higher wisdom and frequently a textbook for psychology courses at universities around the world, has sold more than 10 million copies and has been translated in more than 24 languages.

Make a list of three people you could affect the most with your attitude, wisdom, and life. Maybe your list includes your spouse, children, friends, family members, or coworkers. Who are three people that you could have a positive impact on if you were given only two months to change your legacy.

Next to each person's name, write down the three things that person would say about you if you died tomorrow. Not what you want them to say, but what they would say based on all of your interactions up to this point. Would they view you as "caring," "kind," "a good listener," "supportive," or would they view you differently.

Now write down the three things you would WANT them to say. Some of these things may be the same as the previous list of what they would say. Some things on this list may be different.

Now really look at the lists. If you had only 60 days to make everything on the "want them to say" list a reality, how would you act differently? How would your next two months be different.

Take the next 60 days. They aren't hypothetical. They actually exist. Act differently. Make the change. Remember, the other person does not have to accept the change in you, that's their choice. Your choice is a change in how you choose to take action. Don't overdo it. Don't be fake or cheap or cheesy. Don't think this is about buying gifts or spending money - it may be as simple as a phone call or a text message. It may be as simple as having more patience and remembering why the relationship with that person is important to you.

CHAPTER 7
CHOOSE A BROADER VIEW

Sometimes we wake up in the midst of a train wreck. We're standing in exactly the wrong spot and we're focused on exactly the wrong stuff. As the pieces of our career, our relationship, our confidence, our finances or our health begin to land in smoldering heaps around us, we stand in stunned silence, thoroughly convinced that if there is a tomorrow, it will only suck worse than today.

It's easy to think that the bad times in our lives are the hardest, most painful, persistent things we can imagine. Trouble with that thought is, they aren't.

If you close your eyes and really feel the fear you're feeling, you'll notice something very interesting: you've felt it before. This isn't the first time you've been scared or nervous or let down or broken or sick or wrong. It's just the most recent time.

When you focus too closely on where you are, it's virtually impossible to see where you're headed. It has been said, that you can't drive into the future if you're staring in the rearview mirror. The same is true with our present circumstance. We'll never reach our full potential if we're focused solely on how bad - or how good - things are at this very moment. While mindfulness of the present moment is critical for us to experience our lives and to focus on what we are doing at that exact moment, too much of a stare into the train wreck keeps us from seeing what's happening just a few feet off the tracks where the grass grows through the sidewalk cracks and the sun is still shining.

It's hard to be upbeat and positive when you find out that your spouse is cheating or leaving. It's hard to be happy when you find out that you're being let go from your job. It's hard to be joyful when your investment banker moves to a foreign country with your retirement savings. Fortunately, no one is recommending that you try to "feel" anything. Heck, a little anger, fear, and sadness might serve you well in these situations.

Sadness helps us mourn and then move on from bad relationships. Anger helps us seek fairness - like pushing us to file a police report. Fear makes us seek safety in our relationships, careers, and investments. However (here's the "but" part)... those emotions are beneficial only as long as they're not extended beyond their usefulness. For example, using the fear of being hurt as a guide in future relationships is ill-advised - caution is a good idea but fear is limiting. The sadness of loss is designed to remind us to mourn and honor but when it becomes overwhelming and lingering, it's time to kick it to the curb and replace it with some positive and useful emotions.

When you're so laser focused on the bad stuff that is happening to you, you're unable to look beyond it. Countless times we've seen people who will talk about their sadness, fear, or anger as if it is the saddest, scariest, angriest thing anyone has ever felt. They are overwhelmed by the emotion they have chosen to engage.

If you're caught in the trap of overwhelming emotion, think about the emotion you're feeling - really focus on it. Close your eyes and let that sadness, anger or fear rise up inside of you. Have you felt that feeling before this? Yes, you have. These feelings are quite common. If you can journey back through your emotional history you're going to find other times when you were hurt, or scared, or angry. And in each of those instances, you'll likely find that you that came out of the previous events in mostly one piece.

Maybe you can remember a time when you were much younger and you were home alone. There might have been noises or shadows. Did you hide under the covers? Freeze in the dark wondering if you felt the air move? Regardless, you made it through that scary event. If you'd only have known that you were going to be okay, you probably wouldn't have had such a hard time that night.

Maybe you can remember when you went off to college or got your first apartment or moved out after the divorce and had that first quiet night when you were truly alone. You might have felt like an indoor cat that gets outside for the first time and suddenly recognizes the vastness of life without a ceiling. It can be overwhelming at first but looking back on it now, you realize that you became stronger and more independent through those times. If only you could have known on that one night that life was going to be okay, maybe it wouldn't have been so strange or overwhelming at the time.

There could have been a multitude of events in your life like those events. Other kids didn't play with you and you were sad - but survived. The classroom laughed at your math error and you were devastated - but survived. Your parents fought and the police came and you cried - but survived. All of those times would have been made much easier if you realized that you were going to be okay. Sure, it was going to be hard but you were going to be okay. Things were going to get better.

The first thing to understand is that things are going to get better. Why? Because they do. That's how it works - if you let it. Life has ups and downs. Your job is to learn to enjoy and maximize the up time while minimizing and shortening the down time.

Think about where you are in your life right now - whatever you're feeling - and recognize that if you go ten years down the road into the future, you are going to be able to look back on right now and know that it will be okay. Why? Because it always works that way. You wish you could go back and tell yourself that everything was going to be okay when that scary night happened when you were a kid. You wouldn't have been afraid and it would have been different. That's the same thing your future self would tell the current self in the midst of the train wreck. Just like every time in the past, you're going to be okay.

Some people will say that it's easy for people who aren't feeling the sadness, anger, fear, frustration or whatever to tell them that "it's going to be okay." How would we know? Maybe we haven't been exactly where you are. Many of the people we've met while researching and writing this book have been there - and far, far, worse places - but what about those of us who haven't been where you are right now. How can we tell you that it's going to be okay? Well, we can do that because IT IS going to be okay. There isn't any other alternative. As long as you keep breathing, we'll be able to prove it to you. Why? Because that's how it works.

Life has ups and downs. When you get caught in one of those down cycles, remember all the things you've been through in the past. Realize that like everything you've been through before in your life, everything is going to be okay this time too. Tip your cap to the you of the future - the "you" ten years down the road - who came back to remind you that you are going to survive this too. And when the time comes that the sadness, anger, and fear are no longer prompting you to seek closure, fairness or safety, then you can let them go and turn your mind to a better emotion.

If sadness has run its course, it's time to choose happiness. And if you don't remember how to be happy, just do the opposite of everything you were doing in sadness, it's bound to be pretty close. If anger is just making you angry, maybe you should choose kindness and compassion. If the anger isn't working any more, try volunteering to help people in need. If fear has you afraid to leave the house even though the danger has passed, it might be time to call a friend and go dancing. If your last boss let you go and your lack of confidence has your resume writing skills stuck on permanent writer's block, it might be time to choose confidence and mail a few imperfect resumes to some imperfect jobs just to get your flow going.

Feeling any feeling more, won't make it go away. No one ever got over sadness by feeling more sad. Nobody ever got less angry by being more angry first. Besides, there isn't someone out there waiting to stop by your place and give you a fresh set of "feel good." If somebody offers that it's probably in a syringe, or a bottle, and you might want to pass on it. Even if the person of your dreams has arrived on a gleaming stallion to rescue your broken heart, you're best advised to actively choose your desired feeling before you let them help you find one. Pick what you're going to be, be it, and then get on with happily-ever-after.

A client battling with the fear and sadness of a crumbling marriage was asking how he could fix his relationship. He desperately wanted to keep his wife, who was spending more and more time away from home after a promotion. Long business trips had developed into suspicions of affairs and a growing level of mistrust. He was desperate. When advised to shift his focus from the thoughts of unfaithfulness to instead focus some attention on doing nice things around the house, he perked up and asked, "To make her happy?" "No," we told him. "You can't make her anything. You can't make someone feel anything. She will have to choose happy. You should do those things because you're a good man. Work on being the kind of man that any woman would want to have. Work on being the kind of man that she fell in love with decades ago. Not for her. Do it for you. Fix your stuff. It might not save the marriage but at least you'll come out the other side knowing that you're whole on the inside."

We've got to live the way we should live. Choose to be decent, kind, happy, and whole. Maybe the person who broke your heart won't find their way back to you but you'll be a better person either way. Whatever the train wreck - focus on you and remember that it's going to be okay. Your own history proves that to be true.

CHAPTER 8
IS HAPPINESS A THOUGHT OR A FEELING?

For some people, the theory of being able to actively choose your outcome meets with initial skepticism. The way each of us deal with our emotions, feelings, and thoughts is different. We all go about processing our world in a different manner, so each of us arrives at our decisions and our desired outcomes in different ways. While the process we use to value and determine our desired outcome is different, the fact remains that once we choose where we want to be, we all have the power to arrive at that place.

While it doesn't affect the outcome, it is important to have your own understanding of how you process your decisions. In basic terms, some people are "thinkers" and others are "feelers." This concept is based on the work of Carl Jung and the follow-up work done to create the Myers-Briggs personality indicators.

Imagine you're driving along the highway and come upon the scene of a car accident. There is broken glass, ambulances, fire trucks, smashed cars, and maybe even something covered by a sheet laying in the road. Do you look at the accident scene and try to determine what happened? Or do you look away because you can almost feel the suffering of those involved in the crash?

That's one example of the different ways a thinker and feeler respond. The thinker tends to analyze things using mental processes. The feeler is more connected to the emotions than the actual actions or events and they more easily identify with the feelings of others. There is not a "right" response in these kinds of situations. Being a thinker is not better than being a feeler or vice-versa, but understanding the method you use can help you go about making active choices.

Thinkers may wonder why something like an accident scene bothers someone else so much. A feeler may wonder how the thinker can be so unfeeling about a tragedy with so much pain and suffering. People on the borderline of thinker and feeler may use one or the other method depending on the given situation. Regardless of the way you approach the accident scene, you're neither right nor wrong. There isn't a correct way. It's just the way you've learned to make those decisions.

Thinkers are not devoid of feeling and feelers are not incapable of thinking their way through difficult situations. We all are a blend of both elements, we just tend to lean in a particular direction.

Take the example of a wife walking into the house one day and saying to her husband, "There was a meeting at work today. The company is relocating us to Tulsa."

If the husband is more of a feeler, he's likely to consider how the news "feels." What personal connections will be impacted by the change? Does he love the place they currently live and is he concerned about finding that feeling in a different house or city? How will the kids feel about a move?

If the husband is more likely to make an assessment of the situation as a thinker, he may arrive at some of the same questions, but he will get there in a slightly different way. He may think about the implications or the steps of a move. He may also consider implications of a different home or implications for the children, but he will come at it through his thinking process versus his feelings. While he will easily be able to consider his feelings and the feelings of the kids, he will generally do that by thinking about how something feels.

Once again, neither approach - thinker or feeler - is correct or better than the other. They are just different. That difference is important though because it will affect how each person goes about adjusting the outcome of their decision process.

It's very difficult to change your actual decision process style. It's also unnecessary to change the way you process. Sometimes feelers who encounter difficulty in life will wish that they could be more like the thinkers they know - and vice-versa. Instead of trying to change the process, what each person must learn to do is to assess the process and assure that they are using their process to obtain their desired positive outcome.

Feelers can easily remember a specific feeling, especially the ones they like. Because we all gravitate toward the feelings we value the most, it is entirely possible that you can generate the feeling you are trying to obtain or the feelings that you associate with your desired outcome. If you're a feeler and your desired outcome is to be happier, close your eyes and feel what it feels like to be happy. You can actually generate those positive feelings. These are the feelings that you need to generate whenever you can. As a feeler, you can also allow yourself to feel what it feels like to be wealthy, healthy, confident, or compassionate. If that is your goal, feel it. Feel yourself being successful at it. If you can do this in the quiet spaces between the bigger feelings, you'll develop that feeling as your default resting state.

Thinkers tend to analyze things a bit more and they may not be able to generate feelings as easily. Thinkers compile the facts and make a decision. Thinkers need to focus on the thing they are trying to obtain and then generate the internal facts that they associate with achieving that outcome. For example, a thinker who has actively chosen to be healthy should spend their open moments thinking about what their healthy outcome is like. Think about how you would stand or sit if you were more healthy. Does your posture change with that thought? Think about what you would eat if you were already the healthy person. Does that change your lunch order?

If sobriety is the thinker's intended outcome, think about how that works. What does that look like in the future? How does sobriety sound? Does your sobriety allow you to think more clearly? What does clear thought look like to you? Do you think more clearly just by thinking about clear thinking? Just in doing that, you begin to use your "thinker" preference to begin achieving your desired outcome right now.

It doesn't matter which approach you use for your decision preference but it is helpful to understand which way you go about the process so you can use that process to your advantage. It's a good idea to take a personality test, such as Myers-Briggs, so that you get an understanding of your operational style.

Your decision preferences don't just impact the way you reach a decision, it impacts the way you interact with other people. Thinkers tend to think of feelings as things that get in the way of rational decision making. In having such a view, thinkers will often spend a lot of time trying to get things to fit their very logical view. If you're a thinker, you're more likely to reach your intended outcome through what you see as a series of logical steps. You may also be more critical of yourself and others as you travel the road to your intended outcome.

Feelers tend to check their decisions based on how those decisions impact their own life and the lives of others. Feelers are also more likely to focus on the things that they enjoy and avoid things that they don't like. Criticism is not easy to give or take for most feelers. Conflict is also more stressful for feelers while some thinkers may use conflict to test others.

It's useful to understand your process so that you can understand the ways to guide yourself to your desired outcome. A thinker will want logical steps for changing their thinking while a feeler wants to make sure they feel good about the steps they are taking.

As most music fans will know, John Lennon of The Beatles was a feeler. "My role in society, or any artist's or poet's role, is to try and express what we all feel," Lennon told Playboy magazine in 1980. "Not to tell people how to feel."

Jim Morrison of The Doors was a feeler too. As was Kurt Cobain of Nirvana. You can see how their preferred decision making style affected not only their music but also drove their addictive behaviors and even their untimely deaths. Morrison said:

> "Love hurts. Feelings are disturbing. People are taught that pain is evil and dangerous. How can they deal with love if they're afraid to feel? Pain is meant to wake us up. People try to hide their pain. But they're wrong. Pain is something to carry, like a radio. You feel your strength in the experience of pain. It's all in how you carry it. That's what matters. Pain is a feeling. Your feelings are a part of you."

Walt Disney was a thinker. He came at things from a different perspective than Morrison or Cobain. "All the adversity I've had in my life, all my troubles and obstacles, have strengthened me," Disney said. "You may not realize it when it happens, but a kick in the teeth may be the best thing in the world for you."

Disney was motivated to avoid the pain of more "kicks in the teeth," while Morrison seemed to be pulled toward feeling them more. Both were great men who contributed a legacy to society but they were different in how they arrived at their decisions and they both arrived at their desired outcomes of changing a small part of the world through their work.

CHAPTER 9
THE MYTH OF EMOTIONAL CONTROL

One of the reasons that this book exists is because of an argument. It wasn't a personal argument but rather an online one that we followed while we were reading everything we could find about the topic. Our search wasn't to write a book but rather to find some recommended titles for our clients - something they could read that would let them hold onto their hope and give them some step-by-step ways to change their outlook.

Our search took us to a large online bookseller's review of a book advising people to just "choose to be happy." That was the premise of the book - all 20 plus chapters. The problem was the book never seemed to fully acknowledge the rest of the world. There was nothing more than choosing happiness. Readers noticed. Some readers gave the book low scores and mentioned the fact that there is no real discussion of hardship or pain or suffering. Just be happy. Ready... set... go!

The author of that book believed that it should be possible for everyone to choose happiness and ignore everything else. The author's theory is eloquently explained in chapters of examples and studies. Despite the detail, readers struggled to connect. They seemed to be living "real lives" and reaching out for help - thus the book purchase - but they didn't seem to be able to actually wrap their minds around how to implement that kind of "joy at all costs" process in their day-to-day frustrating, sad or angry situations. They couldn't move past the tough stuff to get to the good stuff no matter how hard they tried.

This book isn't a critique of the theory of strictly choosing happiness. It isn't necessarily a "bad" theory, in fact, for some people it will work - fairly well. You can certainly decide that you're just going to smile right on through everything - no matter what. It is an approach that you can take - and many people have.

In Buddhism, the belief is that happiness is simply the absence of suffering. The author of the book on happiness seemed to propose the exact opposite. And why not? Buddha's philosophical perspective has been studied for centuries by millions of devotees. Wouldn't it stand to reason that the opposite could be just as true as the original? If happiness is the absence of suffering, couldn't also suffering be the mere absence of happiness? Shouldn't you just be able to throw on a genuine smile and decide that your suffering isn't any more real?

Once again, in our opinion, ignoring the bad isn't the best way to achieve the good. While some propose that it is possible, that doesn't make it advisable. It's possible to live for seven days (or so) without food. We just don't advise it. It's possible to stand on the edge of the roof on a 15-story building but that doesn't make it advisable. Swim with great white sharks… possible. Drive 170 miles per hour in your Honda… possible. Decide to ignore the street signs… possible. Those things just aren't the best way to do life for most people. There are the rare people - shark researchers, stunt men, race car drivers - that can pull off the spectacular. There are also rare people that can just slap on the smile and everything seems to happily fall into place for them. The rest of this chapter is for the rest of the world.

Don't ignore your emotions. Embrace them. Feel them. Respond to them appropriately. Having full emotional control is almost impossible. Ask anyone who has tried - really tried. There are people who have spent their entire lives trying to have complete emotional control. A small number of Tibetan Buddhist monks have been successful in achieving what appears to be nearly complete emotional control.

A study of emotional mastery in Tibetan monks by Dr. Paul Ekman, University of California, San Francisco School of Medicine Professor of Psychology, found one monk who could not be startled. The man showed no reaction to sudden very loud noises, including no rise in blood pressure, no jump in heart rate, no change in skin temperature, and no micro muscle movements. Ekman believes the man's years of practice in meditation and emotion regulation caused him to register no significant signs of startle or disturbance.

While we should probably admire the monk's devotion and his stunning success, most of us don't have time for that kind of devotion to emotional mastery. So when we try to control those emotions, we instead do things like suppress them or ignore them, which leads to all kinds of other problems.

Think of your emotions like a balloon. You've got the ability to hold a certain amount of emotion inside without too much difficulty. Over time your emotions become deflated and leak out without you noticing much. That leaves room for some more emotions to go in there. The problem comes when we have a lot of emotions coming at us at once. Those stressful situations where multiple people do things that cause us to be angry or overwhelmed. Those are the times when the balloon is going to fail. Despite our best effort to hold the emotion and control it, we end up with consequences of the ruptured balloon.

You are completely free to choose your feelings. You have certainly met bitter people who respond to everything with bitterness, anger, and cynicism. You could just as easily, following the other book's advice, choose to be a happy person who smiles in spite of the car accident, the cancer, or the thief. But can you really shut down the emotion that powers the natural reaction? We propose that you cannot and should not. It would be like ignoring all the street signs when you drive. Street signs are there for a reason. They help you get where you need to go. Emotions are the same. They exist for a reason.

It helps to understand that some emotions aren't "better" than others. They all exist to serve a purpose - to alert us to something that needs a response.

Anger serves a purpose. Let it serve that purpose. If your auto mechanic is taking advantage of you, responding with a smile while whistling a happy tune and paying the bill is fine if you want, but aren't you going to just carry that anger around? Responding with physical or aggressive anger is rarely advised unless there is real physical danger to life or limb. We're not suggesting you beat up or even shout at the mechanic. This is about understanding that feelings have a purpose and you need to respond to them appropriately. If you're angry, you can still write the check but you can ask questions about the work that was done and you can express your dissatisfaction by deciding not to return to that particular mechanic.

Too many people will tell you that there are "negative emotions," like anger or sadness. That view tends to leave people with the belief that happiness is "better" than sadness. We actually feel even worse when we experience sadness in that belief system. Not only are we sad about what we're feeling, we're feeling the weight of an emotion we believe is a weakness in us.

Get over thinking that there are "negative emotions." There are only emotions and they aren't better or worse than one another. Sure, we'd all prefer to be happy but that doesn't make sadness "bad," or "negative." It strictly means that we have a preferred or desired emotional state. To ignore, suppress, or try to eliminate feelings of anger or sadness leaves people out of touch with their emotions.

Instead of ignoring your emotions, recognize those feelings and act appropriately on them. Don't ignore the anger, rather take the steps to make sure that you are at least recognizing it for what it is - a sign that something unfair has occurred. It's completely possible that you will not be able to jump up in the middle of a meeting and respond to a slight from your boss - even gently. Don't shove it aside though, even if you decide that you aren't going to respond to it because you have a higher value for your career security or your ability to forgive. Recognize the anger, give it due consideration and then you'll be making an active choice about not responding. In this manner, you're making healthier and wiser use of your emotions.

While we can't completely choose to "just be happy," we can certainly make the active choice to be happy. That does not mean that happiness wins out over any other possible emotion, it merely means that happiness is our preferred choice in the absence of the need for other emotions at the moment.

By making the active choice to be joyful, you are setting joy as the filter by which you are viewing things around you. You are determining that you will use joy as a response whenever possible. You must allow yourself to experience all of your other emotions and determine the healthy ways for those other emotions to be acted upon when they surface.

Over time, actively choosing joy will begin to reduce the times that you need to use anger or sadness. As your brain becomes wired to joyfulness, you will find that it is harder for your brain to respond with anger or sadness. That doesn't mean you've suppressed anger and just chosen to smile but rather you have changed the system in your own mind that determines when something deserves to rise above your chosen joy. You have actively chosen joy to be your emotional state until something rises up enough to be addressed.

Don't just slap on a smile and act like things are fine when they aren't. Instead, actively choose to be a happy person who lets the little things go and reserves the need to be angry or sad when things rise to the level that they actually deserve that response. If you adopt that life strategy, you'll find that people will really pay attention when the anger or the sadness comes up in your life because it occurs less regularly.

The concept is the same if you've actively chosen to make being healthy your desired outcome. In doing so you understand that being healthy makes you happy. You also know that being angry or sad is stressful to the body, so you try to spend less of your time in those emotional states. You further recognize that suppressing emotions like anger and sadness can result in health issues, so you choose to act appropriately on the emotions when they appear.

No matter what you've actively chosen to be, you simply make it the highest priority for your emotional usage. Then you respond appropriately to the emotion when it rises above the priority of your chosen outcome. Only when it rises above your chosen outcome does the emotion deserve a response. Your response should have the goal of addressing the issue quickly and directly so that the emotion can be resolved. Once resolved, you can return to focusing on your desired outcome - because it has been set as your highest priority and your default emotional state.

Don't seek to control your emotions, it's typically a losing battle - unless you've got a spare 30 years and a monastery. Instead, seek to control the times in between the bigger emotions and to deal with the emotions when they become a priority.

Renowned as a martial artist and film actor, Bruce Lee found himself edging more into a philosophy teacher in the years before his untimely death in July of 1973. Lee had become incredibly famous after starring in five full-length martial arts movies in the early 1970s including *Fist of Fury* (1972) and *Enter the Dragon* (1973).

Beyond his movie roles, Lee had developed his own fighting style which he named Jeet Kune Do (The Way of the Intercepting Fist). The style was a mishmash of other martial arts but was as much a way of living as it was a way of self-defense.

Lee, who had majored in philosophy at the University of Washington, spent considerable time reading and writing about the best ways to live and process our thoughts and feelings. Even when he was instructing others in self-defense, he was instilling important values such as acknowledging feelings. "You have to keep your reflexes so that when you want it — it's there. ...Not accepting even one inch less than 100 percent of your honest feelings. Not anything less than that. So that is the type of thing you have to train yourself into. To become one with your feelings so that, when you think - it is."

Lee told his students, "Choose the positive. You have choice - you are master of your attitude. Choose the positive, the constructive. Optimism is a faith that leads to success."

As a student of so many different philosophies - Eastern and Western - Bruce Lee pushed his students to always question what they were taught, even by him. Many of his notes on life were published after his death in the book *Striking Thoughts*. In those notes, Lee had written, "The primary reality is not what I think, but that I live, for those also live who do not think."

If you want to begin to take the concept of setting your desired outcome as your resting state, take a close look at one of your typical days. Write down every time you feel an emotion and how much time you spend dealing with it. Now look at all the times in between those emotions. Wouldn't it be life changing and incredible if you could guide your mind during those times to your desired outcome?

Recall what kind of day you were having that day. Was it a "good" day? A "bad" day? A "normal" day? A stressful or quiet or strange day? If you had to rank that day based on how it felt overall, would you say that it was a happy day? Did the day generally move you toward your stated outcome? Did that day reflect your desire to be happy, wealthy, healthy, generous, giving, or sober?

Consider what would change in that day if you made sure that the times in between the bigger emotions were fully focused on your desired outcome. If you made the active choice to be what you want to be during those periods, how much of a difference would that make?

CHAPTER 10
NEUTRAL IS NOT AN EMOTIONAL STATE

On any given day at any given moment, how do you feel? Think about that for a second. It isn't a question of health. It's a question about your emotions. It's generally easy to pick out how you feel at those moments when you feel strong emotions - anger, happiness, embarrassment, and fear - but what about those other times?

Most people understand emotions as either positive or negative. In fact, you can find many lists of emotions that break them down that way (see chart). The challenge is that listing emotions as either positive or negative gives no value to the periods when we may not be feeling anything strongly enough to register on an emotional level. Are we just emotionless at these times? Does nothing exist between the strength of emotions? What happens in the time when we are working and feeling neither happy or sad? Are there moments in our day where we are not grateful or angry? Are there times where we don't feel anything "good" but also don't really feel anything "bad?"

GENERAL LIST OF HUMAN EMOTIONS

"Positive" Emotions	"Negative" Emotions
Interest	Panic
Desire	Disgust
Surprise	Indifference
Hope	Fear
Gratitude	Anger
Joy	Grief
Relief	Frustration
Self-confidence	Embarrassment
Generosity	Greed
Sympathy	Cruelty
Love	Hate

Some people have theorized that the state of "peace" is a common resting emotion but peace seems a bit bigger than "nothing" when it comes to these non-emotional moments. Peace might fit in the quiet non-emotional times but there seem to be too many people in today's fast-paced world that are standing in the middle of their busy days without really feeling much - but definitely NOT feeling peaceful.

We would propose that these neutral or seemingly emotion-free moments are actually the most important parts of our lives. They are important because we can choose to fill them with the desired outcomes that we want. This is the time where making an active choice matters the most.

But what does that look like? How do we generate a feeling when we aren't otherwise feeling anything? How do we remember to do that? And does it have any lasting effect?

Recognizing these moments comes down to being in tune with your emotions and being able to identify them - or rather the lack of them. We've already stated clearly that the emotions you're feeling are signaling you to provide an appropriate response - and you should respond to them. If you aren't actually responding to any emotions, you should be using your inner attention to direct your emotions. When you aren't feeling anything, you should be creating the emotion that you want to feel. This is actually the time when you can choose to smile, choose to dream, and choose to change.

These less emotionalized times provide a great opportunity for us to step into our happiness, our hope, our desire, our interest, and to get things moving in our favor. If you're not feeling something... choose to feel what you want to feel - choose to feel who you want to be in the future.

At first, you'll really have to focus on these quiet times and turn your attention toward creating the feeling of your desired outcome. It may take time to train yourself to feel wealthy, healthy or happy but consistently doing this over a few short weeks will train your mind to use the feeling you're inserting as your default resting emotion. Eventually, your mind just begins to fill the non-emotional times with the feelings that you want.

The great thing about this process is that when you begin to automatically fill the non-emotional times with the feeling you actually want, it begins to seep into the other times. If you're constantly feeling happy as your default resting state, it takes longer for anger to show up. It also takes a more motivated and meaningful anger to break through the joy - which means you're only responding with anger when it is actually something worth responding to in that way.

If you need help remembering to fill those moments, it can be really useful to have reminders. Some people have success with personal reminders - such as colored silicone bracelets or a special piece of jewelry or a personalized pen. Hold that item in your hand and focus on the feeling you want to generate. Now visualize that feeling entering that item - really fill it up with health, wealth, peace, joy, or whatever.

Some people need more visual reminders such as signs, computer screen savers, and a storm of sticky notes. Write down what you're going for and feel it when you see the sign or notes.

We've worked with people who have ordered specialty items of all kinds from online print shops and used those items to keep their minds focused on the thing they are trying to obtain. It doesn't have to be expensive, it just has to be a good reminder for you.

If you struggle with how to feel wealthy during those down times, close your eyes and imagine yourself in that Lamborghini or that big house. That's the feeling you want to feel all of the time. The same goes for healthy, just close your eyes and picture yourself at your ideal weight or completing the marathon you have in mind. That's the feeling you want to feel all of the time.

We're frequently asked if this kind of thinking works for a few days or is it something more permanent. Will reading this book get you going in the right direction only to find out that the first speed bump knocks you back into a bad cycle?

As you begin to fill your world with the feeling of the thing you're trying to achieve, you're going to be amazed at how you begin to actually attract the things to you that help you reach the desired outcome. When you feel the end result of your goal, you'll bring the goal closer to you.

When you spend your quiet moments focusing on feelings of joy, you're going to attract joyful people and joyful events. Your joyful thoughts will build on joyful thoughts. If you're desired outcome is to be happy, then beginning the process of filling your quiet moments with feelings of happiness is the best way to start. After time when it becomes habitual to have joyful thoughts, you'll discover that filling your quiet moments with joy is also the best way to already be there - in your happiness.

Moving toward desired outcomes such as health, wealth or becoming a veterinarian can take more time to reach but having the feelings of wealth, health, and veterinary success before you get there is kind of like "greasing the skids" or "paving the way" for the end result.

When you spend your quiet moments experiencing what it feels like to be the vet you've always wanted to be, you'll find that your mind begins to think like a veterinarian. And when your mind begins to think like a veterinarian, you do better in school, you make better decisions about your veterinary future, and you begin to weigh everything else in your life against whether it feels "vet-like." Everything you do - from decisions about spending your time to decisions about purchasing things - gets framed around how they lead to the desired outcome. Everything you do begins to make you the veterinarian you want to be in the end.

This can be a big concept for people. Start small. Just close your eyes and focus on what it feels like to be that person you are going to be down the road. Every time you get the chance, do that again. What do you really want more than anything else? How will life be when you get there? That's the feeling you're going to want to use over, and over, and over again. That's the feeling you want to make an automatic habit - a resting state feeling of your desired outcome.

CHAPTER 11
HOW TO BECOME POSITIVE

Simple things that seem obvious can become difficult to explain. If something is obvious, it requires little thought or analysis to accept, whereas complicated things have multiple points along the way where an analytical person might find reason to question things. The problem with explaining something that may seem obvious is that you end up stretching out and adding multiple argument points. With all that in mind, we are going to try to explain something obvious and point out why it's true: To lead a positive life, you have to have positive thoughts. Seems obvious, right. But there's so much to the concept that it's worth a closer look.

To begin with, having positive thoughts is about generating positive thoughts. You have to make the choice to think positively. Let's understand "thoughts" a little bit more.

Recent scientific studies suggest that the human mind - yours, mine, everybody's - has somewhere between 50,000 and 70,000 thoughts each and every day. For the sake of the discussion, let's take the middle number and say that people have an average of 60,000 thoughts each day. That's 60,000 thoughts regardless of what you're doing. You have virtually the same number of thoughts regardless of work or play.

Your brain has a function - to think. It generates thoughts whether you're resting and daydreaming or in the middle of doing your taxes. The thoughts it generates are different for sure, but the number of thoughts is relatively steady.

For many people, there is a group of thoughts that they have that are negative, regardless of the situation they are in. They find themselves looking in the mirror and thinking, "I am fat," or thinking about talking to another person and thinking, "maybe they won't like me."

Take a second and think about the things that you think about yourself, your body, your personality, your future, your present, your past. Be honest and really focus on those thoughts. What is the worst thought you have about yourself?

If you really focus on the things you tell yourself about who you are as a person, you'll find out that many of those thoughts are not true. Even the thoughts that may be based on some past failure often arrive in our mind based on faulty information and a screwed up delivery system.

As an example, let's take a look at something like seventh grade. There isn't anything much more traumatic in the lives of many people than the awkward teenage years. At some point during this time, many of us attended a school dance where we mustered up every ounce of self-confidence and courage we possessed and we asked someone we liked if they wanted to dance with us. They may have laughed when they said "no," or they may have said they weren't interested in dancing with us.

This is where our problem starts. We wonder if we are not good looking enough, not popular enough, not a good dancer, or whatever. All of that self-confidence we had is washed away. We begin to walk through our lives with a pile of doubt. We can't ask attractive people out, they might turn us down and then we'll feel bad again. We give up dancing.

So many people begin a string of "failures" because they lost their mojo at a young age. The life that follows even gets some people so bogged down that it affects decisions about whether they go to college, use drugs, or even contemplate or attempt suicide.

As most parents know, the seventh grade example is fraught with problems. If you've ever had to talk your kids through the process of dealing with rejection, you know that the person who said "no" to the dance, may have just been unable to dance and unwilling to admit it. The no-giver could have been surprised by the request and unable to say anything else. Maybe that person was shy. Maybe that person thought we were out of their league - too good a dancer or too attractive - and so they said "no" because they didn't want to embarrass themselves. Maybe that person's friends didn't have anyone to dance with so they said "no" to minimize their friends' loneliness. There are a lot of scenarios where the person who said "no" didn't even factor us into the equation when they turned us down. What if that person didn't really mean it when they said "no."

But what if they did? What if they didn't like us? What if we were too short, too heavy, too boring, too much acne, or whatever. Frankly, seventh graders are a really bad judge of character, so we probably shouldn't have valued their opinion that much.

Think about it. What if you walked outside right now and ran into the local twelve-year-old boy from up the street. If he offered his unbiased opinion of your haircut, wardrobe, or lifestyle, you'd probably ignore him. Even if he got really jumpy and decided to tell you that you are ugly, fat, or stupid, you'd probably grab him around the collar and ask him if he had a mother you could speak with about his attitude. You wouldn't put much value in the statements of a twelve-year-old these days... but we sure did hang onto those same faulty opinions back at the time.

All that soul-crushing angst from seventh grade - or whenever it was in your life - was untrue. It was probably poorly filtered by our mind because it didn't consider the other available motivations for the rejection. Or maybe it was delivered by a bunch of fragile kids whose opinion shouldn't have been trusted. And in spite of all of the flaws with the experience and how we interpreted it, we developed a series of neural pathways in our mind that were really good at handling our rejection.

If the dance experience or one like it made us feel fat or ugly, we now had a strongly established pathway for handling all of our body-image thoughts and feelings. Each time we had a negative thought, it just reinforced the strong connection our bad experience had etched into the neural paths of our brain. We began a habit of our negative thought. Those powerful negative pathways began handling every thought we have about our body. Eventually, negative thoughts seemed to pour from our mind automatically, no matter how much we tell ourselves to "stop thinking that way."

When we spend a lot of time having negative thoughts, we become better at generating negative thoughts. Thinking, in that regard, is just like anything else we do. If you shoot baskets all day, you get pretty good at it. If you cut hair all day, you get pretty good at it. If you think about your shortcomings all day, you get a lot better at that too. When our brain is familiar with the negative, it gravitates toward the negative. It begins to fill the spare gaps of time with negative thoughts because they are familiar. Our brain is more likely to respond to all kinds of stimulus and inputs with a negative response - because the responses are familiar.

Even if someone is kind to us, our brain is so accustom to negativity that we are likely to reject a compliment. The very structure of our minds makes it so that we minimize or discard things that are positive.

How many times have you told someone, "You look nice today," or "what a wonderful meal," only to have them suggest that "you're just saying that," or something else that lessens the compliment? When our mind becomes trained to the negative, even the positive is hard to accept.

New research is even finding that when we are in a negative frame of mind, we are producing and emitting a negative energy. The negative energy is likely to attract additional negative energy and to actually repel sources of positive energy. You feel this dynamic when you are happy and around people who are angry - it's a lot of work to stay happy in that environment, so you may want to move away to avoid that drain. Angry people tend to attract other angry people. Negative attracts negative.

It isn't just that our negativity is attracting negative people, it is also attracting additional negative events to us. Have you ever noticed that when one thing goes wrong, it seems to cause a cascading effect of bad stuff? If you've ever had a day that "went from bad to worse," you've probably experienced this phenomenon. Some people even refer to this phenomenon in ways such as Murphy's Law. Murphy's Law suggests that "if something can go wrong it will." While the law is sometimes a tongue-in-cheek way to be less stressed when something breaks or goes wrong, it's also based on the strange reality that if you're rushed, pressured, or stressed, bad things tend to find you. And that's just true.

The great thing about understanding all of these things about negative thinking and the ability of negativity to multiply exponentially and attract more negativity, is that the opposite of all of these things is also true.

If you begin to think positively, you're going to create positive neural pathways and you're going to project positive energy. You'll build a mental state that rejects negative comments just like the negative mind was rejecting compliments. That's right, you can actually inoculate yourself against negative thoughts just by creating a strong habit of positive thought.

When you start your day by saying that it's going to be a good day, you're actually creating the positive mental state to attract positivity. Smile. You've got the ability to make good things happen - seen and unseen.

People are drawn to positive people. They want to be part of that energy. When you draw people to you, opportunities arise. Think about being a salesperson and instead of repelling people with your sales pitch, you've got them coming up to you and wanting to hear what you might have to say. Sound far-fetched? It's not at all.

You can create such a strong and positive vibe that nothing can knock you off your game. We're not suggesting that nothing will ever go wrong, that's not necessarily true. What we tell people is that they can improve their own lives and their perspective so much that the small things won't bother them, the big things won't knock them down as hard, and the people around them will notice.

It's possible that you could never have another negative thought or have another negative thing happen to you if you could just go hide in a cave. If you could find that place where nobody else's bad energy came close to yours. And that's the rub, right. You can't live in a cave. You have to have a job or whatever. You can't just avoid the boss and she can't avoid you - even if you're filled with positive energy and she's full of anger, the time will come where you're in the same room.

Regardless of your level of positivity, you're going to be banging around in the world with other people who may have different energy. This means that you'll never be completely free of bad things. There's too much random on the freeway, in the grocery store, and in the genes of the human body. Stuff happens. But by developing a solid positive mental outlook, you'll attract more positive and you'll be better prepared for bad things that might occur.

The other benefit of positive energy is that you'll eventually change the people around you. As people are drawn to positive energy, they are also moved by the strongest energy sources around them. By becoming the positive energy in your office, you'll eventually change the dynamics of the office, or your home. Positive parenting will generate positive children. Being a positive partner will get you a stronger relationship.

Remember, you didn't develop those negative pathways overnight. It takes time to turn things around. Start by telling yourself some positive stories. Make some positive affirmations and repeat them over, and over, and over. Those 60,000 thoughts that you have each day are going to be there either way. If you start repeating positive things about yourself over and over, you'll fill in the gaps before your mind can fill it with negativity. It might take a little practice at first. That's okay. Learning anything new is a process and this is no different.

If you're used to telling yourself that you're fat when you look in a mirror or see your reflection, change the story. Say "I'm hot," "I'm looking good," or "I really like the way I'm headed," over, and over, and over. It isn't necessary to even believe it at first. Just start saying it. The negative stuff isn't true either. You just said it enough that it became true. You just let that "fat" label bring with it all the negative energy that goes with that and your body responded by keeping you headed in the wrong direction. Turn your mind... and your body will follow.

For a month or so, you might wrestle with saying something positive every time you look in a mirror. Keep doing it. The world's hard enough and it won't be cutting you any breaks any time soon, so you kind of owe it to yourself to say some nice things to yourself. If you're walking around waiting for someone else to tell you how great you look, then you could be waiting a while. Maybe there's some seventh grader up the street handing out free opinions and maybe this time it will be different than in the past - want to take that chance?

Tell yourself the positive stuff. Tell yourself that every day starts as a good day. Will they all end up that way? Ours did. But it took believing and it took time.

You've got some brain training to do and you've got to overcome all that negative stuff that has been sitting on your doorstep for far, far too long.

In a study published in 2007, Psychology Professor Ellen Langer of Harvard University and psychology student Alia Crum (now a psychology professor at Stanford University) published a study detailing the interesting effects that the mind can have on things like personal health. The two met with 84 female hotel maids from seven different hotels. They assessed the maid's health variables that are affected by exercise - weight, blood pressure, body fat, waist-to-hip ratio, and body mass index (BMI). The maids were then divided into two groups. One group was educated about the fact that their work - cleaning hotel rooms - was very physical and exceeded the Surgeon General's recommendations for an active lifestyle. That group was shown how their jobs made them physically active and their work counted as exercise. The second group received no such information and was monitored as the "control group."

Testing done four weeks later showed that, when compared to the control group, the members of the educated group - with no changes in actual behavior - showed decreases in weight, blood pressure, body fat, waist-to-hip ratio, and body mass index. The only difference cited by the study's authors was the fact that one group became mentally aware that they were actually exercising every single day.

The study's authors conclude that exercise definitely affects health but the mind plays a role in how much of an effect occurs. That's pretty powerful positive thinking - don't you think? Remember where we started this chapter. To lead a positive life, you've got to have positive thoughts. And that's obvious.

CHAPTER 12
THINGS THAT MAKE US CHOOSE

You've probably noticed that life can get "interesting" sometimes. There is always somebody out there trying to "push our buttons." Even when people aren't trying to force us to do something, there may be situations where God, the universe, or Mother Nature has a surprise in store for us.

Regardless of how well we have our current situation under control, we're constantly banging into stuff that seems out of our control. Someone else does something and our controlled world suddenly has a dose of chaos, drama, or stress. Even when everything is running smoothly, it may seem like we're always one dishwasher leak or late-night phone call away from our next round of pressure.

All of the stress, drama, chaos, pressure, urgency, disarray, turmoil, and unexpectedness that we face tends to push us to make quick decisions. It's important to recognize when those things are driving the choices we make because we've got to make our active choices in a thoughtful and conscious way.

It's completely understandable if the stress of your job is pushing you to actively choose a new path. That's what this book is about, right? The thing that you d⌐

want to do is to be driven by a stressful situation into making a bad choice.

A friend of ours explained an interesting phenomenon in her job. She works as a rescue coordinator for the military in the waters off of the Hawaiian Islands. Often times, she explained, a ship captain in trouble will transmit a desperate 'mayday' radio call for help and then almost immediately begin making terrible decisions which further increase the danger of the situation.

Making bad decisions under stress isn't just the domain of frantic ship captains. Drowning swimmers have been known to drown their rescuers while in a state of panic. People lost in the wilderness will often traverse dangerous terrain even though rescue is more likely if they just stay put. There are hundreds of documented events of so-called "friendly fire" where soldiers have been killed by their fellow troops during chaotic battle conditions.

While people make bad decisions when stressed, it's also true that indecision in a stressful situation can lead to undesired results. Freezing at the moment of decision has also lead to plenty of tragedies on the seas, in the wilderness, and on the battlefield.

The more we dig into decision making under stress, the more we find problems. We can't trust that we'll make the right decision. We might make not only a wrong decision but a decision that makes our situation worse. Or we might not make any decision and things will decline more rapidly.

So, the questions become: How are we to make a wise active choice for our path in life if we're caught in the middle of a stressful time? How can we be sure that we're making the right active choice? How can we be sure?

It would be easy enough to say: "We can't be sure." But that's a bit simplistic. We can be sure that we are making the right choice. We just can't be sure that the outcome will be exactly what we think it should be when we get there.

Let's back up a bit. To make a good active choice we've got to turn down the noise. We've got to be able to take the stress out of the situation. Keep in mind that most things that lead us to need to pick a different positive outcome for our life didn't start up overnight. We don't find ourselves instantly unhappy, instantly poor, instantly overweight, or instantly out of touch with our family. And even if something catastrophic has occurred that changes your reality overnight, the decisions that must be made are generally beyond just the sudden occurrence. People with a cancer diagnosis, a sudden divorce, or the death of a child, are often making active choices to change their outcome but they generally find that the shocking event opens their eyes to many other things in their reality that need to change.

When we understand that our current situation took some time to create or that our current situation extends beyond just a single catastrophic event, we can allow ourselves a little time to contemplate our active choice. Is the choice we're making something that really comes from inside of us? Is it a choice that feels right - not just for this situation - but for our entire life?

The first rule of active choice in the middle of your storm is: slow things down. Don't RE-act to a situation but rather ACT upon the entirety of your life to move to something different.

The second rule of active choice under stress is: breathe. Studies of those situations where people make mistakes, when drowning, lost, or in a firefight show that the mistake-maker is functioning with limited oxygen supply to the brain. The human body responds to stress with muscle tension. The result of stressful muscle tension or constriction in the shoulders, neck, and chest is that breathing becomes more shallow. Shallow breathing results in lower oxygen supply to the heart and the brain, which prompts additional stress and impairs decision making.

If you find yourself in a critical place trying to make a significant decision, remember to breathe deeply. Give your brain some oxygen. Breathe - that's rule number two.

The final rule of dealing with the drama and trauma of the things swirling around you is: Stress doesn't exist. Only when you remember that stress doesn't exist, do you feel better, right? Wait. What? Stress doesn't exist?! That's a tough concept. When we talk about stress not existing people tell us that we obviously haven't... had high-pressure jobs... raised teenagers... had to decide between having food in the fridge or paying the mortgage... had a boat trailer tire blow out on the Interstate while going around a corner at 65 miles per hour... gone through a divorce... had someone in our family die... dealt with a health issue such as cancer... or whatever.

Yet we have done all of those things - many simultaneously. Some of those situations were hard, undoubtedly. They were even stressful at the time. In spite of all of those situations leading to us feeling stress, we have come to realize that stress itself doesn't actually exist. It isn't a "thing." You can't buy it or sell it. You can only perceive it. You can only sense it lessening or increasing.

Sure, some situations trigger your "fight or flight" response. They elevate your heart rate. They make you sweat. They prompt you to respond - right now. These things that trigger this response can even last over an extended period of time - which can take a physical toll on our bodies. Yet, you can do something to contain it. You have the ability to control your reaction. If you can control your reaction - if you can lower your heart rate, breathe, fend off the sweat, and pause the fight-or-flight reaction - you can avoid the response that we all call stress.

The best people in the world of business, sports, politics, entertainment, and war know that they "win" by being more in control of their stress than "the other guy." Stress for them isn't a negative thing - it is a motivator. And the only difference between them and us is the way in which we perceive stress.

There are many good books out there that focus on reducing stress or even converting it to a motivator. For our purposes in this chapter, we merely want you to be able to recognize your reaction to stress so that you can assess whether you're making a bad selection in response to your stress or whether you're making an active choice to change the things in your life that are causing the stress.

If your life is currently being defined by chaos and you're interested in making an active choice to do something or be something different, remember the three rules for active choice under stress:

1. Take a moment to make the decision.
   Act versus react.

2. Breathe. Give yourself the oxygen to make wise choices.

3. Remember that stress doesn't exist. Only our reaction exists and that can be controlled. Slow things down enough to allow the stress to be a motivator - not a generator. Be motivated to move forward not caused to move out of fear.

For too many people, stress and drama become distractors. Stay focused on your desired outcome and you'll find that a lot of the external noise that comes from other people and outside events will quiet down. The little things that used to seem big will fall by the wayside once you've made your active choice and can begin living your best life.

CHAPTER 13
CHOOSING THE BAD

We've all known someone who was a negative person. In a cynical world, there's always someone who seems to be trying to set the record for cynicism. You could give those people a sunny day with a blue sky and they would complain about the heat. Add a raincloud and they'll be sure to hate that too. It seems there is no pleasing those people. They've firmly developed a habit of negative choice.

If you think about your feelings and your outcomes as a choice, the world gets a bit more complex for a while. It takes some time to wrap your mind around the fact that everything we think and feel really is a choice we make. The good is just as available as the bad. The happy is just as readily available as the unhappy. The joy is just as available as the angry.

Make a list of what it takes to make you angry. Write down the things that really make you mad. Now, make a list of what it takes to make you happy.

If you've done the exercise thoroughly, you've probably got a good pet peeve list of bad drivers, spousal nagging, lazy children, overbearing in-laws, incompetent co-workers, and poor customer service on the angry list. The happy list might have things like puppies, promotions, sunsets, love, money, walks on the beach, or other things. But really compare the lists. If you're like a vast majority of the people in the world, the angry list is filled with smaller and more tangible things than the happy list.

The angry list is filled with the things that people do "to" you while the happy list is a compendium of things that you have to do, achieve, notice or appreciate yourself. We allow our circumstances to dictate our negative existence while we must generate our positive existence. It would seem then that we should be a happier bunch of people, right? If all we have to do to claim our happiness is notice the sunsets and work hard for that promotion, wouldn't it be the best way to live? And yet, too often, we choose the alternative. We stand around waiting for everyone else to ruin things for us. And we never seem to get the things that we deserve.

Let's take a different look at your list. Just focus on anger and happiness for a second. Close your eyes and feel anger. What images do you use to create it? Or does it come up naturally for you? What colors and temperatures do you experience in anger?

Open your eyes. Look up at the ceiling or the sky. Think about pizza. Now close your eyes and focus on happiness. Do you generate images? Or does happiness rise up naturally for you? What colors, temperatures, and images do you experience in happiness? For many people, anger is easily generated. It is red, and it is warm, or even hot. Happiness tends to come in greens and blues and you have to focus on places in nature or a calm scene to get you there. The difference is that we have become good at generating the negative emotions but must rely on something external to generate the positive emotions and feelings. Our emotional generators are wired exactly opposite of the way we want them to operate.

The good news is that these habits are relatively easy to change. Your mind can learn to generate positive responses instead of negative responses. It's about choosing to be happy - choosing to generate those good feelings instead of the negative ones.

Good feelings are just as readily available to you as the bad ones. Think about the fact that anger and happiness don't really exist. They aren't tangible things that you can hold in your hand. Just like with stress, you cannot go to the store and buy more angry or happy. They are emotions that must be generated in order to exist. For you to be angry, you must become angry. For you to be happy, you must become happy. You must generate these emotions. If you must generate them, you can choose which ones you want to generate.

Over the years, you've developed reflexes that help you generate those emotions quickly. A cute girl or guy smiles at you and you smile back - happily. A person bumps into you in the grocery store and you tell them to watch where they're going - angrily. Our experiences in life have honed and automated our emotional responses. Because we've experienced good things and bad things before, we become more skilled at generating the emotional response. But we ARE generating that response. It requires an initial choice - even if it begins to feel involuntary.

It is certainly possible to angrily respond to the smiler or to happily respond to the person who bumped into you. We've actually all seen examples of those kinds of seemingly "odd" responses. You can probably recall times when you witnessed someone responding angrily to a kindness or someone responding with a smile to a situation that you would have responded with fury.

We are not seeking to turn your emotions upside down. Just because it is possible to respond joyfully to an unfairness, doesn't mean that it is the correct response. Remember, all of our emotions serve a purpose. Anger exists to protect us from wrongdoing. There is an appropriate time for it. What we are suggesting is that you can choose the appropriate response when needed and you can also choose to use the most beneficial emotional response for you.

Anger is useful when it protects you. Does anger benefit you in any way when the person who cut you off in traffic is already driving away? Do you angrily speed after them to give them a piece of your mind? Tailgate? Angrily recall the story of the bad driver to the first four people you see when you get to the office? Do any of those responses fill the appropriate need of protecting you? Speeding after the person does the opposite in most cases. Tailgating isn't much of a protection but we've all seen people respond that way, even with their family in the car. Does carrying the anger all the way to work and sharing it serve a purpose other than to increase and extend the emotion?

When your mother calls and offers her analysis of the way in which you should live your life, you can choose to be angry or sad. Many people won't respond with that emotion directly to the person causing the issue but instead will end the call and carry the anger somewhere else. They will complain to their spouse, yell at the dog, or go lay on the couch and cry. And yet that anger and sadness are serving no real purpose in that instance. And you're having to choose to generate that emotion. You're using your reflexes to generate the emotion and then delay a response. Even if anger, frustration or sadness are appropriate responses, if you delay them until after the call, they are serving no purpose. If you do angrily tell your mother that she is being unfair, you may have appropriately used anger to respond to an unfairness but once the call ends, what is the benefit in remaining in the anger? What is the benefit to YOU of staying angry?

Are we suggesting that you can just turn emotions off and on, like a light switch? Frankly yes, because you can. Once again, though, we aren't suggesting that you turn on inappropriate emotions and turn off the appropriate ones. We're suggesting that you learn to identify the emotion when it appears, respond in an appropriate manner and then move to an emotional state that serves you best for the moments that follow.

Anger has prompted great changes in our society. If no one became angry about slavery, prejudice, and discrimination, there would be a lot more of it. If no one became sad about the tragedies of starvation, disease, and homelessness, there wouldn't be many people and organizations striving for an improvement. But think of the people that are prompting the changes after they feel the initial emotion.

Dr. Martin Luther King Jr. actively chose to lead a civil rights movement with peace and forgiveness. His anger and frustration were there. His outrage and fiery passion were there - in his words and his actions but he was not an unhappy, angry person. He wasn't angry all the time - quite the contrary. You find many happy moments when you study the man or listen to those who knew him. His anger appropriately fueled a desire to change an unfair situation but it is not the emotion for which he became known.

Mother Theresa was called to serve in the worst slums in the world. Her sadness at the things she saw prompted her to take action but she did not walk around in that state of sadness. She actively chose to walk around with joy and she shared it with every single person she met. She brightened lives. She gave joy to people who had no reason to generate their own joy. She showed them how to experience happiness in a place where none should have existed. Sadness was her motivator but it never became her master.

Those are two extreme examples. No one is expecting any of us to be the next great humanitarian - unless you actively choose to be. However, we can all learn from and understand the value of appropriate emotional response. We can all learn the real value of choosing to live our lives at the most appropriate level of emotion for us.

When we CHOOSE to leave the anger as soon as the moment of danger or unfairness passes - as soon as the perpetrator is gone - we are making the choice that we would rather be something other than angry. We are recognizing that being happy, joyful, confident, secure, and peaceful draws more positive things to us than the negative alternatives. We are also recognizing that we are in charge of the things that we feel.

When we walk through our days maximizing our positive emotions, we begin to find that we are indeed happier. We are better people. We are better parents. We are better spouses. We are better workers, bosses, and colleagues. We begin to motivate the people around us to bring out THEIR positive emotions. By elevating the positive emotional output of the people around us, we begin to change our corner of the world.

CHAPTER 14
FEELING ALIVE

From time to time you may run into people who are remarkably angry. We aren't talking about people who are mad about something that has just happened. We're talking about people who have a constant boiling rage that surfaces at the smallest infractions and explodes at anything else.

A client once told us that he felt like the anger was lurking constantly just under his skin and he struggled daily to control it. He explained that his anger was so intense that he actually feared it. He also reported being exhausted every night from fighting all day to suppress and control his own emotions. Yet when faced with the opportunity to give up his anger, he offered an interesting thought: "I'm not sure who I will be without my anger. I hate it, but it makes me feel alive."

In the end, the client was able to successfully learn techniques to not only let go of his constant anger but to learn to feel all of his emotions and respond to them appropriately. He reconciled with his partner and, at last contact, was focused on a job promotion which offered him an interesting future career path.

The angry client's statement about anger making him feel alive seemed surprising when we first heard it. As we began to look deeper at our other clients we found that some of them, when asked the right questions, would admit that their negative emotional experiences and responses where the ones that had the most meaning in their lives. Indeed, many felt like the "normal" them - without anger, sadness, guilt, or fear - was not very worthy or very interesting.

It's a unique dilemma. If you want to actively choose something other than the overpowering emotion that has made you legendary in the office or in your family, are you running the risk of not becoming relevant in that group? Is it possible that the angry manager at work would have never become a manager if he wasn't so outspoken - and angry? If everybody didn't feel bad for poor, suffering Suzy over the holidays, would anyone notice that she was there?

Even if Suzy wants to be joyful or the manager wants to be nicer, it may be difficult for them to see themselves without the usual behaviors. If your negative feelings are the only feelings, you may consciously or subconsciously fear making a change. In fact, your body and your mind can keep you from making changes.

As humans we're wired to resist change. Our body keeps a constant temperature, maintains our pH balance, and uses hormones and chemical processes to regulate sugar and calcium balances in our blood. Our muscles become accustomed to the activities in which we engage and new exercises may be painful as the body resists a change in routine.

The mind is also working against us when we try to change. Our brain builds neural networks to support reoccurring thought patterns and makes it difficult for new thought patterns to take hold. Our subconscious remembers every time we've failed in the past. Our autonomic nervous system triggers an increased heart rate, sweating, or many other reactions when it senses that we're stepping into stressful territory.

While we're afraid of making changes for fear we will lose "ourselves," and our body and mind are working against change, we've also got to factor in that the people around us may not want us to change - even if the change is better for us.

The angry manager has a reputation to live up to and even though people fear him, he may be effective in getting things done. Sometimes the higher-ups want a hatchet man - they need somebody who can "do the dirty work." They may be resistant to the angry manager trying to be a happier person - even if the angry manager has had one too many ulcers and a heart attack because of his personality.

What about Suzy? She's been sad for so long that she's surrounded herself with a network of sad people and rescuers. She knows exactly which friend to call when she's having which kind of trouble. The people she has brought around her are rescuers. They may actually have really crummy lives but they feel okay about those lives because they've always got Suzy to show how bad it really could be for them. Suzy's sad network of "friends" might not much care for Suzy's active choice to find a little joy in her life. It may seem strange to think that the people around us could be cheering for us to stay the same miserable person but it's a very common occurrence.

We worked with a client once who was a single mom, raising two kids by herself for more than a decade. She had great support from her co-workers. They bought her thoughtful gifts on her birthday and they made sure she could have time off to handle sick kids and school functions. When she met a great guy, they were happy for her - at first. When that great guy became a serious relationship and the single mom was floating around the office in love, suddenly the girls in the office realized that this person they had "helped" so much didn't need them anymore - in fact, the woman's life was suddenly filled with the love that they were all lacking at home. Jealousy ensued and the single mom found her job on the chopping block. She was stunned at first and wondered what happened to her "friends" in the office.

Wow! There sure are plenty of challenges if you're really an angry or unhappy person committed to making a new active choice for your life. You could fear losing your identity. Your body and mind could fight the change. And the people around you might try to hold you back.

This is exactly the kind of situation where the power of active choice is necessary to make the change. There isn't room to "try" to be a better person. There isn't time to "attempt" to do better. It's time to just step into your intended outcome. It isn't time to tell people you're trying to be nicer. Too many people fail when they try. Decide your outcome. Make the active choice to be nicer or to be happy. Because when you become nice or you become happy as a person, there is no going back - regardless of your own mind, your own body, or all the people around you. In fact, by the time they all figure out what's happened, there is a very good chance that you'll have made a habit out of being the 'new' you and you might just have trouble changing "back."

You see, the answer isn't to make small steps. The answer isn't to begin "one thing at a time." No, if you're tired of being angry and have decided that you want to be kind, then make the active choice to be that person. Step into and start being it. You don't have to take a training course on being kind - even if you've never been that before. There's nothing served by trying to be kind to one person at a time or in one situation and not others. It's far easier just to step into being kind. If you've actively chosen to be a kind person then go about your day in that way. When you actively see yourself as a kind person, you begin to make the daily decisions that support that outcome.

The next time you find yourself feeling like your job doesn't challenge you or your spouse doesn't excite you anymore, realize that you're merely working out of a belief that is leading down the path of anger, resentment, and sadness. Choose to challenge yourself in your job. Choose to love your spouse unconditionally. Choose to be the person that you want to be and let the other stuff sort itself out. Make an active choice to be better, healthier, wealthier, wiser, or whatever.

CHAPTER 15
LIFE... IN RETROSPECT

Living your life in today can be tough enough. Watching out for tomorrow can be exhausting. But by far one of the worst mistakes we make is spending time wishing things would have been different in the past.

It is pretty easy to develop a significant case of "developmental bitterness" when we're spending our time wishing for a different past. There isn't a single thing you can do that will change anything that happened in the past - and that includes five seconds ago, five days ago, and five years ago. You can wish all you want for better parents, a different choice that one time in high school, a different marriage or a different conversation with someone else, but there is nothing to be done that will change it.

Of course, we can - and should - apologize when we do something wrong to someone else. And we should always try to correct the errors in judgment we ourselves have made. It's always best to correct our own actions and mistakes. What we're talking about is the people who are either trying to correct someone else's wrongdoing or simply wishing that things hadn't turned out the way they did. Every second you spend wishing to change the past, is a second you are wasting in your future.

Looking back on all the things that we might change if we had the chance, only serves to make us bitter. We become less satisfied with the things we have when we realize that they could all be better "if only..." something had gone differently.

Some people wish away their present by wishing they'd had rich parents or maybe wishing that they had hit a home run instead of striking out that time the scout came to watch us play. Sure, life would be completely different if you had dated so-and-so and if only you had taken that job at Apple when it was still in Steve Job's garage.

If your current life includes a replay movie of the decisions you made that could have been different, then you need to start watching a new movie. There is not a single thing you can - or should want to - do differently right now to change the place you are right now. Let those things go. Repeating the story of who we could have been is nothing more than writing the fictional outcome to the many paths our lives could have taken. You're just putting a happier ending on those other movies than the one you think you have right now.

It is completely conceivable if you had made a different choice that the outcome of that path could have been different than what you think it would have been. What if you'd won the lottery... and got hit by a bus, or poisoned by the unknowingly greedy person you could have married. What if you'd become a major leaguer... with the same alcohol problem you have right now. Would the huge fall feel better? And would you still be sitting where you're sitting right now?

What if your destiny is to be exactly where you are right now? What if your destiny is about what you do over the next three months? Six months? One year? What if everything in your life hinged on the things you decided in the next few days? If you knew that your destiny was in the future - not the past - you would turn your attention to making the best future possible, instead of trying to figure out how the past mattered. The movie of your life is not made up of moments in the past - good or bad. The movie of your life is still being written and you have the opportunity to decide what it will be like.

A lot of people understand the concept of the previous paragraph. Read it again. The concept sounds really good, but if your life is spinning out of control, how are you going to stop the spinning long enough to grab a tiny piece of stable ground? If you're ready to stop living in the past, you'll need to focus on the present and the future.

There's something important in that key paragraph back there. It says that you have the opportunity to decide what the movie of your life will "be like." That's different than saying that you have the complete control over what the movie will be. It's important to understand the difference. If you have chosen to go live in a cave in the remote woods of Canada for the rest of your days, you'll undoubtedly have a great deal more control over the rest of your movie.

Of course if you're like the rest of us, you've probably got a job, a family, friends, a place to live, and much, much more. You can control your "role" in the larger movie but the actions of other people, outside events and all those other things are out of your control. No matter what you do, at some point in your life, some other person's movie is going to come crashing into yours. There is no way to prevent it or ward it off, short of that cave. The best you can do is keep moving forward and stay focused on what happens to you next. Focus on how you grow and learn and move forward, and give up the things you've encountered in the past.

Remember, you can't drive a car forward if you're constantly staring in the rear view mirror. That's just truth - regardless of business or life. Our past may define our present but that doesn't mean that it will define our future. Letting it define our future is a choice that we would have to make.

No matter how successful you have been thus far, the old saying says that "you can't rest on your laurels." And you can't. Just like all the good you've done doesn't matter much moving forward to bigger and better things, the bad things that have been weighing you down don't matter either.

It doesn't matter if someone in seventh grade told you that you were fat, stupid, ugly or smelly. That person was wrong - even if you WERE a big kid who made silly mistakes and had unfortunate skin and body odor. You're the only one who has the ability to permanently define yourself using the adjectives of the past. That kid doesn't get the right - unless you give it to them.

Sure, you could have gone on to great riches if you'd bought that Microsoft stock in 1993. Yes, your life could be better if you had more money, more time to spend with your family, better teeth... whatever. But you didn't buy that stock. Thinking about it now is only beneficial if it causes you to buy the next great stock. However, most people will do the same thing they did back in 1993, which is to buy a pepperoni pizza, a new television set, or a six-pack of Heineken. The reality is that there are thousands of decisions you could have made differently in your life but the only one that counts is the one that you will make next.

Looking back on any choice we make - even the smallest ones - and wishing we had chosen differently is a losing proposition. It has no real benefit. If we learned from a mistake, then we've gained the requisite knowledge to not repeat the event. Everything else is just wasted time in the present which equates to wasted opportunity in the future.

If you're reviewing the past, then you're living in the present with buyer's remorse. We've all done it - bought a big TV or the latest cell phone, only to determine that the purchase wasn't worth quite what we paid for it. No matter how hard we try, the picture on the TV never looks quite as good in your living room as it did in that store. No matter how many calls you get, there's still an annoying echo sound in the earpiece. And now that you have that car - everybody else is driving one too.

If you should have married Mary instead of Linda, then spending your days thinking of Mary is probably not serving you or Linda well. So, you've got to make a new choice. There are plenty of options (in fact an infinite number in this scenario):

1. You could ditch Linda, get a divorce and go find Mary. Maybe she's as miserable as you are these days.

2. You can spend your days hating being married to Linda and wishing she would do something differently to make you happier. Maybe she even feels the same way about you.

3. You can decide that maybe Linda was a good option for you, buy her some flowers and see if you can't figure out what made you pick her in the first place. Who knows, maybe Mary's a bitter old lady by now and at least Linda puts up with you.

Beyond the above choices are a bunch of others, especially when you throw in the fact that Linda and Mary also get to make choices as well. There's the real possibility that Linda and Mary would have made different choices if you had made different choices. Your different choices could have brought Suzy into the mix of possibility and she could be better than Linda and Mary. Or Suzy could be a serial killer. You probably shouldn't spend much more time thinking about it.

You can spend as much time as you want playing out the different movies but it really doesn't change the fact that you've got to be focused now on what you're going to actively choose for your future.

CHAPTER 16
IT'S NOT ABOUT YOU

Are you someone who gets their feelings hurt a lot? Do people talk about you behind your back? Are you sure that everyone at work is gossiping about all of your failures in life? Did an acquaintance say "no" to a coffee invitation last week and you're trying to figure out what you've done wrong?

When we are children, the world seems to revolve around every boo-boo, every trophy, every art project, and every gold star. As we grow older we may develop a sense that everyone is truly interested in our achievements. Extending from the idea that people care about our small victories is the idea that people care about our defeats and our faults.

Maybe you've encountered someone who told you about their breakup, their layoff, or their medical problem in the same breath that they were introduced to you. They were quick to explain their faults and they may even assume that you've already heard about them and their shortcomings. This person is an "up-front-er." They usually believe that you will dislike them eventually just like their last lover, last employer or own body and so they are telling you up front about all of their problems.

You yourself may have done this at some point in your life. You may have done it with the last person you met. You might be able to look at yourself and think,

"Wait a minute, when did this become me?" When did you go from being that happy person to being this person stuck in the rubble of their failed relationship, career or life.

What about the person who is carrying around a huge secret or failure of their own making. They may even move from town-to-town or job-to-job as soon as they believe that people have discovered the felony, the promiscuity, the anger problem, or the addiction in their closet. People often wear their shame and pain so outwardly that they're sure everyone can see it. Someone forgets to return their phone call or turns down an invitation to lunch and the person instantly assumes that the other person has discovered their secret and wants nothing to do with them.

Do you worry constantly that other people don't like you? When someone at work walks past you quickly in the hallway with only a nod, do you wonder if they've talked to someone else in the office about 'that thing' that happened last February?

Paranoia is the symptom that frequently develops when someone is "up-fronting" or hiding something. We become so obsessed with our own fears, faults, felonies, and failures that we walk around thinking everyone else can instantly see them, know them, believe them, and dislike us for them.

This is a place where many people just get stuck. They are a "failure." Whether they are 25, 35, 45 or 75 years old, they're thoroughly convinced that the movie of their life has been made. The things for which they will be known have already been determined. For these people, the future holds only groups of people who will grow to dislike them as much as they dislike themselves. They are stuck in the past and stuck in the present and they are spinning their wheels, digging deeper, and deeper into the rut of personal paranoia.

And what if it isn't paranoia? What if people do know something about your past? What if everyone knows your failures? Is there any way to move on from something when it happens in a small town or in the office? This is a critical area where active choice matters most.

People will adopt your interpretation of your past. That's not to say that you need to provide the excuses, the defense, the gory details of everything you've ever done wrong - quite the opposite. The first step when everyone knows about your failure, is sometimes just admitting that you're human. Recognizing your failure and redefining it as a strength will make others view it in the same light. If you realize that you are stronger than you were before the failure, then other people will begin to sense that strength. Even without explanation or apology people will see that you have moved on, and they will too.

We've all made mistakes. That's just true. Perfect people don't exist. They are a myth. We're all broken sometimes. Some people decide to move past their mistakes. We can learn from the mistakes or we can let them define us. Either way, it is a choice. We have the ability to choose to not let those past failures define who we are today and tomorrow.

The world is a forgiving place. Heck, we cheer for the underdog constantly. Rising up and moving on is a badge of honor. The trick is that you have to be able to move on. You can't keep dragging all those failures around. They're probably very heavy.

If you're going to make the active choice to be something… then you're going to have to also make the decision to stop being the other thing. This is true regardless of the desired outcome you've selected. If you've actively chosen to be healthy, then you're going to have to stop being unhealthy. You're going to have to give up the unhealthy behaviors. If you're going to live wealthy, it means that you're going to have to stop making decisions like a poor person.

The hard part for some people is letting go of the past. If you're sure that everyone else is "making you miserable" with their inability to see you as the happy person you've passively decided to become... then you're stuck. Passively choosing something and expecting others to go along with it because you say it is true is the problem. You're counting on your happiness being accepted by others and you're counting on them buying in, forgetting your past mistakes, and liking you regardless.

In active choice, the other people don't matter. Well, they matter but they don't get to decide. Instead, you're choosing to be happy regardless of how they act. You're actively choosing the outcome based on how you want to live - not how they expect you to live.

Go ahead. Tell us all the reasons that just being what you want to be isn't going to work. "Well, I was in prison for four years and everybody else keeps bringing up my felony. How am I going to be steadily employed and happy, much less wealthy?"

First, you're going to decide to be happy. You'll have to actively decide that you've moved past whatever bad happened and you're ready to do what it takes to arrive at next.

"But nobody will give me a break. I can't get a job because of my felony conviction." We've had this conversation with several clients. We end up pointing out that they seem to be the ones who keep bringing up the conviction. Sometimes we wear our past like it defines us instead of wearing our present like we define it.

Don't get us wrong. There are many employers out there who won't hire convicted felons. It isn't our place to say whether that is 'fair' or not. In their business, they can make those decisions. You may have to work harder than everyone else but if you've actively chosen to be happy while you do that work... then it's going to be a lot easier.

If you've failed your family with alcohol and you feel like you're spending most of your time apologizing for past mistakes, then it might be time to ask yourself who is having the trouble moving on. Apologize and move on. You've made the active choice to be sober. Live that sober life. We're not saying everyone is going to forgive you for the horrible stuff you've done. Your wife might not come back. Your kids might be afraid of you. Those are their choices - and maybe they're even justified choices. The important thing is that you've chosen to be sober regardless of their choices. You must actively choose the path you're going to walk. Let them choose their path.

"But will it all work out? Will I ever be happy again?" And there it is again. You can't actively choose to be happy and then leave everything on everybody else. They don't make you happy. They don't make you drink. They don't make you use. They didn't make you a felon and they don't make you an ex-felon.

Are you going to be happy again? Yes. As soon as you actively choose to be happy - regardless of what's going on in your life. You're going to be happy as soon as you actively choose to fill your quiet calm moments with joy. Take some time to laugh.

Are you going to be a firefighter? Healthy? Wealthy? A rock star? An artist? Yep. As soon as you decide to be any of those things. Start making decisions like you've already arrived. And be the person that leaves the past behind. Everybody else moves on unless you keep acting in the broken manner that is part of the person you were in the past.

If the people at work need to talk about you, make the active choice to give them something to talk about - such as "wow. Have you seen how Joe is walking around here acting happy all of a sudden?" The novelty of your happiness will soon wear off. If people need to be upset about that, we recommend that you keep right on smiling - not because they're talking about you but because you don't have time to notice now that you're focused on your own active success.

If you need some help overcoming your own traumatic past deeds, here's an exercise: Write down the five biggest mistakes you've made in your life. You can mention other people as victims but stay focused on your role in the mistakes. Don't blame your "bad friend" Jimmy or your ex-wife or why the drugs were to blame. This is about the five biggest mistakes that YOU made. Now write down the lessons you learned from those times. Write out why you know that you would never make the same mistake. Write down how you're different, stronger, and more wise. That is experience. That is wisdom. Wise people are not failures.

If you can explain to yourself how you've learned from your mistakes, then you need to recognize that those mistakes were experiences that made you stronger. In fact, those things led you to this point in your life. Your mistakes might just be the things that made you strong enough to decide to make a change - to live that better life that begins with actively choosing to be something else.

It is not your job to rid everyone else of their impressions of you. They will have to do that themselves. Your job is to begin forging a new impression by walking boldly ahead like none of those other things define you. What defines you now is the active choice to be happy, to be healthy, to be strong, to be wealthy, to be filled with compassion, to be a hair stylist, an architect, a poet, whatever.

You can't tell everyone "move on, because I have." That's not your choice. That's their choice. You don't get to demand that they get over your mistakes just because you've chosen something else. We're merely suggesting that you stop giving them the opportunity to punish you for your mistakes through your own actions. Choose what you're going to do. Actively choose what you're going to be. Then move forward with the passion of a person who is already the thing that you want to become.

CHAPTER 17
PUTTING IT ALL TOGETHER

Much of the material in this book is designed to help you understand WHY it's important to make an active choice and along the way there has been some information about HOW to make the active choice. Less of the book has covered the functional process of active choice - until now.

This chapter is designed to help the reader see how active choice might look in action. Of course it's different for everyone but the following sections will explain a bit more about specific choices and offer an example of someone we know who made such a choice.

HAPPINESS

Happiness is one of the key themes of this book because so many people have come to us trying to figure out how to become happy. They want to stop being miserable and they're often looking for a magic map that charts the course to Happy-land - a mythical place where they see other people living but that they cannot find themselves.

It can be a bit anticlimactic to discover that happiness is not a place but rather a state of mind. It is a state of mind that is achieved when we make the active choice to be happy - and in doing so let go of all the things that we thought were preventing us from being happy.

If happiness is what you're seeking, make the decision to be happy. Remember, as explained previously, this isn't about "acting" happy and waiting for something to go wrong. This is about realizing that you deserve to be happy. You were born to be happy. Anything that goes wrong along the way in life doesn't actually take away your happiness.

The limiting belief most people have is that they believe happiness is the absence of sadness, anger, or any other negative emotions. That's only true for the emotion of happiness - not the active choice to be happy. Happy people can feel sad. Happy people can be angry. They recognize that all emotions need a response. They allow anger to prompt action and sadness to prompt appropriate grief. The difference is that truly, actively happy people return quickly to their joy after they appropriately respond to the other stuff called life.

Our happiness isn't derailed by tragedy, drama, and stress. Our happiness can only be derailed when we let tragedy, drama, and stress outlast us and control our lives beyond the appropriate level.

An example: let's call this person Mary came to us because she was devastated by the death of her mother six months earlier. Mary had quit working and was unable to leave the house most days. She actually cancelled her first appointment - twice. When she did arrive, she was so distraught that much of the first session was spent with the tissue box. Mary knew that her grief had outlasted the appropriate time for her to deal with it but she was unable to shake it. Mary's problem - at its very core - was that she didn't realize that she had the power inside of her to stop. She'd always relied on her mother to help her get over things. Her mommy had kissed her boo-boos when she was small. Her mother had eased her heartbreak when boys were mean. Her mother had paid for an attorney for Mary's difficult divorce. Suddenly when Mary's mother died, Mary found herself without the person who she thought was the only one with the power to make the pain stop. We showed Mary that the power was hers and it had been all along.

If you want to be happy, go forth happily. What do happy people do? Hmmm. Happy people whistle sometimes. Maybe you've seen happy people sing along with the radio while stuck in traffic. Happy people have been known to smile and wish others a "good morning." You may not know how to whistle. Your singing may be poor. But the quality of those things don't matter. It is the quantity of them that makes the difference.

HEALTH

Most people are trying to be more healthy. Stop trying. Just do. You know the right things to eat. Have a vegetable. Eat a smaller portion. Exercise. There are thousands of great books out there that can point you in the right direction. The reason that so many people fail at being healthy is because they are still TRYING to be healthy.

If you're going to take health into your own hands, you have to actively choose to be a healthy person. Some people ask, "How does saying I'm making an active choice to be healthy make a difference when I've been trying everything for years without success?"

Once again. Stop trying. Quit jumping from diet to diet. Just eat better because you have actively chosen to be someone who cares about what they put in their mouth. Walk because healthy people walk. Ride a bike because you want to not because someone tells you it's 'low impact exercise.' When you stop trying to be healthy and instead just actively choose to be healthy, it makes a tremendous difference.

A client we will call Dave was a moderately overweight American male. He wasn't sedentary or obese. He was just busy. He ate things he liked and he drank a beer or two in the evening or on game day. Dave's wife worried about him and inside he worried too. His father was overweight and in poor health. Dave wanted better. He tried a few different diets. He tried finding time to walk at work during lunch.

Dave eventually became frustrated and sometimes depressed about his weight. He told himself that his genes were probably what was holding him back despite all of his healthy attempts.

Dave made the active choice to be healthy after hearing his wife's doctor give her some advice on diet and exercise. We worked with Dave and he decided that he was done trying and was just going to do it. Dave began to see himself as his target weight. He made walking a priority that work fit around because he was a healthy person not a worker trying to squeeze in something healthy between meetings. Interestingly enough, Dave's boss noticed that his attitude at work improved and his productivity increased as he engaged in healthier living.

In less than six months, Dave lost 20 pounds. He feels optimistic when he looks in the mirror. Dave used to grab a burger for lunch from a fast food joint up the street from his office. Several months after his last session, Dave told us that he was pressed for time and decided to squeeze in a quick burger at that restaurant. He told us that it tasted terrible, sat in his stomach like a greasy rock, and he wondered how he'd ever eaten them before. Dave's healthy. He chose to be.

WEALTH

Everyone who thinks about actively choosing to be wealthy asks us if it's even possible to become wealthy just by actively choosing to be wealthy. The answer is simple: yes - at least it's the best possible way. It's rare to get there by luck alone. Today's wealth requires thinking like a wealthy person. This isn't the 90s where a dot-com startup lands you unlimited wealth. This isn't the 60s or 70s where you can just get a "good job," work hard, and retire with enough money to live a nice quiet suburban life. This is NOW. In order to be wealthy, you've got to work smart. You've got to invest - and re-invest. You've got to have a little luck. You've got to constantly think like a wealthy person. Thinking like a wealthy person involves actively choosing to be wealthy.

Remember, actively choosing wealth doesn't mean that it just magically shows up in your bank account. If that's your gig, you may have choice confused with prayer or the lottery. Actively choosing wealth means aligning all of your choices in life around the desired outcome. When you realize that every decision you make must be made with your future wealth status in mind, you stop doing things that poor and middle-class people do - like buy a daily latte for $5. When you're just starting out, you might take the bus to save $10 a day in gas and parking because you know that the $10 can be invested in your business concept, real estate, or your portfolio.

We first met Darryl (fictitious name) when he was 26. He was fresh out of the University of Hawaii with a degree in business. He was teaching surf lessons, holding down a lifeguard job, waiting tables on the weekend and setting up a surfing mobile app. He came to us because he felt that he wasn't achieving his business vision fast enough.

Darryl was working hard - that's for sure - but he'd fallen into the trap of believing that hard work was the price to pay for future success. He was right about the hard work but he was working on the wrong things. Darryl had a vision for his startup app business but it had fallen to fourth on his priority list behind paying for a nice condo, a nice car and an expensive girlfriend. With our help, Darryl downsized the condo to a studio closer to the famous waves at Waikiki, ditched the car for a moped and a bus pass, and convinced his girlfriend that she could still love him while he went through his "broke phase." The changes allowed Darryl to dump the weekend waiter job and spend more time on the app project. Now he was working hard with more focus on the things he wanted.

Darryl's app project is under contract to be purchased by a major surfing equipment company. We'd bet he'll get to that goal of wealthy very soon.

One word of warning - don't assume that "wealthy" is equal to "all about the money." Many people who actively choose to become wealthy find their greatest success is in learning that living with very little can actually make you wealthier than living in excess. If you appreciate the things you have, you don't need more. When you don't need more, you start feeling wealthy a lot sooner. Maybe that's cheating but it's a great way to cheat.

LIFE AND CAREER GOALS

If the active choice you're making is to achieve a life, activity or career goal, then active choice is an exceptional way to go. If you want to be something, get started doing it. If your goal is to be a writer, write. Write for a local magazine or website. Write just to get your stuff out there. Don't write for the money - write because you're a writer.

If you want to be a lawyer, start thinking like a lawyer. Hang out with lawyers. Read about legal rulings in your community. Sit through court proceedings. Immerse yourself in the law and start studying for that law school entrance exam or the bar exam or whatever is next.

If you're a high-school baller with dreams of being in the NBA, put your entire focus on the goal. Practice, practice, practice and keep the grades up so you can get into a good basketball college. Live your goal. When people ask you what you want to be - look them in the eye and say, "I'm already what I want to be - a great basketball player. I'm just working hard to take it to the next level."

If you want to be a rodeo clown, go to the rodeo and hang out with the clowns. Get known enough that you'll be the first guy or gal that they turn to when somebody comes up sick or injured. Get to being the clown instead of clowning around trying to be one.

If you want to be a firefighter, make the active choice that it is your primary goal. A recent client asked us why we told him to tell himself, "I am a respected firefighter," over and over throughout the day. We explained that he could keep competing with the 200 other people who were taking the test each time and 'trying' to get on with the department or he could start thinking like a firefighter.

Once he bought into the concept and started thinking of himself as a firefighter, his test scores improved, his physical training ramped up enough to pass the fitness tests, and he said he felt like he wasn't nervous at all and he just "fit in" with the firefighters who were on the oral interview panel. We wave at that guy sometimes when we pass the fire station on our morning walk. He's a firefighter - because he became one in his mind before he got the job.

If you've spent your life hoping to be something, you should probably recognize that 'hoping' isn't serving you well. It's time to be. And that's the secret of active choice.

Select your desired career. Yes, you've still got to do the work to pass tests, get certifications, get published, get a scholarship, or get hired… but all of those things get a lot easier when you think like the people who already have the job you want.

OTHER CHOICES

Some people desperately want to be confident. Good news - you are. It's right there inside of you. Think about one area of your life where you feel confident or something you did in the past where you were confident. Why are you confident in that area of your life but not in other areas of your life? Often times, we'll talk with military officers who give orders to people all day but come to see us because they lack confidence in the other parts of their lives. It takes a little work and maybe a few mental tricks but these people learn that they are exactly the same person in the uniform and out of it. The uniform doesn't have confidence sewn into it. The person just steps into a feeling of confidence when they put the uniform on. You can do the same thing in any area of your life - if you actively choose to do so. Chose to give your next presentation with confidence. Stand up and knock it out of the park.

Some people come to us because they want to be well. Their active choice is to be healed or to be free of symptoms or pain. Can you really make an active choice to overcome a physical illness or disease? More and more research is finding that you can - especially if you've been diagnosed with a condition where a doctor says "we don't know a lot about (insert your condition here)."

We aren't saying that you should skip the doctors. Modern medicine is powerful and getting better by leaps and bounds. Do everything you can medically to make yourself well, but if you're truly going to be well, then it's time to get your mind on board with the desired outcome. Make the active choice to be well. Do the things that people that are getting well do. Research. Meditate. Use hypnosis. Take the first steps. Pray. Exercise. Drink more water. Ask your doctor, your physical therapist, your oncologist... whatever... if there is more that you can do to be well. Do those things. This is the part where you stop sitting around waiting to die or to receive the miracle. Whatever is going to come next, you should know that you made the active choice to do everything in your power - however limited - to be well.

A client we will call Caroline came to us because her doctor told her there wasn't much more that he could do for her back pain other than a very risky surgery she wasn't willing to undergo. Caroline didn't sleep much because lying in bed was too painful. She had taken to sleeping in a recliner in the living room. She reduced her shifts at work and she was considering going on disability - despite the fact that she would be giving up a job she loved and the only reason she got any exercise at all. Our job was to convince Caroline that she had more power than she previously believed. She had to stop waiting for someone else to fix her back and start living her life the best she could. She had to actively choose to push herself harder at physical therapy and in the pool each day. Before long, Caroline was swimming in the ocean every day before work. She found that she was more relaxed when she arrived at work and she was more tired each night. In fact she was exhausted from the hard work she was doing to get well. Caroline was so exhausted that she started sleeping in her bed for at least part of the night. Once she saw that she had the power to make progress, there was no stopping Caroline. She had made the active choice to be well.

There are probably a million other things that someone could actively choose to do. Maybe you've got something you've decided to choose. Go do that. Actively. Wrap your life around it like there is no other option. Think like the person you want to be. Live like that. You'll probably find yourself where you want to be - or who you want to be - far more quickly than you ever imagined possible.

CHAPTER 18
THE ACTIVE CHOICE F-WORD

Failure. There, we said it. We just don't believe it exists. It's another one of those things - like stress or drama from earlier in the book - that doesn't exist, at least it doesn't exist in the way most of us think it does.

When you embark on any journey in life, there's a possibility that life itself will change around you. You've got to be able to adapt and adjust. You also have to be able to bounce. While active choice will get you where you want to be more quickly and with fewer opportunities for things to interfere - especially your own thoughts - the possibility of not getting there will always exist. Just keep in mind that the possibility of not getting where you want to go DOES EXIST but failure DOES NOT.

Failure is only a defeat if we choose to define it in such a way. There's a much better choice. Choose to see the times where you fall short as an opportunity to learn and an opportunity to grow stronger.

Thomas Edison invented the lightbulb. Pretty amazing stuff if you think about how having light has completely changed our world. He also invented motion picture cameras, audio recording devices, electrical generation systems, portable batteries and hundreds of other items. In fact, Edison still holds the records for most patents by a person - 1,093.

Edison wasn't just good at inventing things. He was very good at failing to invent things. In order to develop the small filament that generates light inside a bulb, he experimented with thousands of materials. Edison was later asked how he dealt with the numerous failures along the path of invention.

"I have not failed," Edison said. "I just found 10,000 ways that won't work."

That wasn't Edison's only valuable insight on failure. He also said, "Many of life's failures are people who did not realize how close they were to success when they gave up." Giving up, he famously said was our greatest weakness as people. "The most certain way to succeed is always to try just one more time."

Of all the things that Edison invented in his life, the most important thing he invented was the proper perspective on failure. For Thomas Edison there was no such thing as failure. It did not exist. Each effort existed to inform the eventual success.

You can actively choose to be healthy, wealthy, happy, or whatever. Actively choosing will get you there more easily - but it isn't a guarantee. We all have moments in our life where our desired outcome feels distant or even unobtainable.

It is in these moments that some might call "failure" where active choice is most valuable. When we set our mind to the desired outcome, then the things we encounter can be viewed more as learning opportunities, speed bumps, or detours along the journey to our destiny.

Has a sudden divorce or death of a loved one made you feel like your goal of happiness is suddenly gone? Has a layoff at work made you believe that your path to wealth is further off than ever before? Did a surprising diagnosis take away your hope for health? If any of these things has happened - don't give up. Keep moving.

Active choice is a destination that is constantly changing, growing, and even becoming better. The things that we all travel through along the way are important reminders that we must continue to strive toward the destination.

There is no failure. There is only life. And the destination is not changed by life, only the path is changed.

CHAPTER 19
WHAT HAPPENS WHEN IT HAPPENS

What happens when the day comes that you have achieved the goal? You've accomplished what you wanted to accomplish. The desired outcome is a reality. You are wealthy… or healthy… or happy… or a train conductor. Is that the end? Can you put active choice on the shelf never to appear again?

The first thing you should do is appreciate the achievement. Enjoy it. Remember where you started and the things that made you choose this moment. Feel the feeling of succeeding. You'd be surprised how many people achieve great things only to not value it much because they get a bit too greedy and turn immediately for more. Or maybe they achieve their goal and it doesn't feel good anymore because they've begun to dream bigger. Either way, when you get to the destination, take a few moments or a few months to appreciate it.

The next important step is to express gratitude for the achievement. Expressing gratitude to the people who helped you along the way helps maintain a stable foundation for your new situation. Gratitude also helps keep you humble. You've achieved something, so be thankful.

Part of being grateful is giving back. You've done something. It's something amazing if you think about it. How many people do you know who have tried to become a writer, or to get healthy, or to become happy - only to fail, time and time again. If you've accomplished something, there is always a benefit in helping others achieve the same thing.

Some people worry that helping others creates competition. Viewing it that way means that you believe that what you have achieved comes from scarcity. Scarcity thinking will hold you back from achieving whatever is next. Remember, there is an unlimited supply of happiness, health, wealth, and every other thing. Help the next person. It will lead you quickly to the next level. Teach others. Show them the things that got you here. Share the resources. Share your insights. Tell your story. Inspire others. Shine a bit. Write down your lessons learned.

While you're doing all of those things, start thinking about what might be next for you. Is there really an end to happiness, wealth, health, or your career? Do you now want to grow those things or discover new things?

If you're ready for the next active choice decision, remember to step into it. Just step into that next thing. The next goal will be achieved before you know it. Never give up. Keep growing. Keep learning. Keep pushing yourself for whatever is next. If you've made it to healthy... wealthy... happy... whatever... then maybe it's time for you to actively choose to be... more wise... stronger... more generous... well read... a motivational speaker... more caring... more courteous... more humble... a stand-up comedian... a world record holder... more faithful... more politically active... an inventor... a rescuer...whatever. Your next is calling.

ABOUT THE AUTHORS

Randy Hampton is a professional writer, consulting hypnotist, social scientist, blogger, and sought-after public speaker in Hawaii. He walked away from a six-figure career in public affairs to find his passion helping people find their passion. He is a former broadcast news director, talk show host, and stand-up comic.

Beverly Craddock is a certified life coach, master hypnotist, brand strategist, consultant, and marketing guru with a Master's in Business Administration. She has worked with people from all walks of life to help them dream big dreams and live out loud. Her experience includes non-profit management, corporate public relations, and public-sector communications.

Made in the USA
Lexington, KY
09 July 2015